THE TUXEDO WARRIOR

CLIFF TWEMLOW

FOREWORD AND EPILOGUE BY
GEOFF THOMPSON

SUMMERSDALE

First published 1980 by City Major Ltd.
Photographs Howard Glyn Rowlands

Copyright © Geoff Thompson 1995

All rights reserved.

No part of this book may be reproduced by any means, nor transmitted nor translated into a machine language, without the written permission of the publisher.

Summersdale Publishers
46 West Street
Chichester
West Sussex
PO19 1RP
England

A CIP catalogue record for this is available from the British Library.

Printed and bound in Great Britain by The Book Factory, London.

ISBN 1 873475 46 2

Front cover photo of Cliff Twemlow taken from the film G.B.H.

Foreword

By Geoff Thompson

When I first wrote *Watch My Back*, an autobiographical book about my own life as a nightclub doorman, I believed that it was the only book of its kind, certainly on these shores. It seemed however that I was wrong. I was informed by my friend Peter (Consterdine) that a man by the name of Cliff Twemlow had previously published a similar book, though it had been out of print for some time. I tried to obtain a copy of Cliff's book but to no avail. It wasn't until some four years later that another friend, Steve Gumbs from Liverpool, managed to get hold of a second hand copy of *Tuxedo Warrior* for me. I read it and loved every page.

Watch My Back had/has been a very successful book for me though I could never quite work out why or what people saw in the book, that was until I read *Tuxedo Warrior*. All the way through I drew comparisons with my own book and saw for the first time what others had seen in *Watch My Back*. I felt an immediate affinity with its author, with his life, his loves and his battles in a city (Manchester) that could quite easily have been my own city. I liked the book so much that I made inquires about acquiring the copyright. Peter, who knew Cliff when he was alive, put me in touch with some of his old friends and relatives, in particular Cliff's nephew Aaron and his life long friend Steve Powell. Aaron had a chat with the family and they very graciously allowed me the copyright to re-release this great little book.

One very sad thing was that I never got to meet the very charismatic author of this book, who died in 1993. It is my hope that in re-releasing this book many others will be able to share

Cliff's fascinating story and gain inspiration and knowledge from a man who lived such a full and colourful life.

Other than adding the Foreword and Epilogue, I have left the *Tuxedo Warrior* as it was written. The words, expertly crafted, are all by Cliff's own hand.

Dedications

First and foremost I dedicate this book to the memory of Cliff Twemlow.

To Cliff's late mother and father Ethel and Harold.

Thank you especially to Aaron, a real gentleman.

To the very charismatic and humble Steve Powell.

To Cliff's good friend Stuart Hurst.

With respect, to the former ladies in Cliff's life, Georgina, Beryle, Judith and Jackie.

To Cliff's sons Dave, Barry and Steve.

Also to his brothers John and William and sister Ethel.

And, to anyone that knew Cliff.

Also, and as always to my own wife Sharon.

Special thanks to my daughters Kerry and Lisa, and my wife Sharon for helping me transcribe *Tuxedo Warrior* onto computer for re-publication.

Preface

Although *The Tuxedo Warrior* is presented in the form of my autobiography, I would consider it a privilege should it be accepted as a literal tribute to all members of this sometimes hazardous occupation (and I am sure there are many who have suffered equally if not more than I) who though subjected to certain indignities, still maintain pride and proficiency in what I myself term to be a noble profession, where courage, intelligence, discretion and understanding are just a few of the necessary attributes required to perform the duties of, to name a few descriptive titles - Doorman, Crowd Controller, Supervisor, Bouncer, Warden - my own personal preference being The Tuxedo Warrior.

The Tuxedo Warrior is a humorous, sad, violent, vulgar and true story.

Contents

The Young Warrior..9
The Summer of 52..15
Chaser..32
Homeward Bound..38
Sassenach Warrior..40
The Army Game..47
The Composer..49
The Sexual Seventies..57
The Omega..63

AUTHOR'S NOTE

Whilst this is a true story some of the character names and places have been changed to protect those not wishing their identity to be revealed, and to protect the author from libel action.

The Tuxedo Warrior

Chapter One

THE YOUNG WARRIOR

I was born on October 16th 1936, at Number 14 Lord Street, Hulme, Manchester, the final addition to a family of six - brothers John and William and sister Ethel named after my mother and myself Cliff.

My father Harold was a strong, powerfully built intelligent man, who spent much of his life away from home, his occupation being a Merchant Seaman. Frequently he would return to dominate our home and lives, causing my mother a great deal of unhappiness and distress which would also affect us. Father was also a self-confessed atheist whose home spun philosophies were in later years to hold a certain profoundness and wisdom for me.

He was often heard to quote 'If there is a Holy Spirit or a devil it is drink, for it can bring out the best or the worst in people.'

Drink was the only religion he believed in and one which he frequently practised. Omar Khayyam, the Persian Philosopher, was my father's Prophet, for whenever the opportunity arose he would encourage us all to read his works. You may say we were weaned on bread and jam and Omar Khayyam.

My mother Ethel, once a chorus girl with the George Roby Troop, was kind, loving and gentle. Her love and knowledge of music, which each of us seemed to have inherited, was to be of great significance to me during the course of my destiny.

Looking back now, the environment to which I quickly became accustomed was a constant fight for survival - street fighting and hardship were accepted as normal everyday occurrences. A once upon a time when shoes were considered to be a status symbol, when going bare foot had to be tolerated by the majority who, in spite of their existence in squalor and poverty, managed to survive the ever increasing hardships of a country soon destined for war.

Germany, who was ready and restless, began flexing its muscles in a show of power. Soon the whole of Europe were to become engaged in the preliminary bouts of war before Hitler made the final bid for world dominance. Britain accepted the challenge and with little more than courage, khaki and blue, set forth to suppress the might of the Hun to the accompaniment of *We'll Meet Again* and *Roll Out The Barrel*.

My father changed services from Merchant to Royal Navy, where he became an Unarmed Combat Instructor and during the course of his career he led silent raids on strategic positions behind enemy lines, engaging in hand to hand fighting with the opposition.

Meanwhile my mother had managed to acquire a more acceptable dwelling for us in Barton, a small village that bordered Eccles, Salford. So, one Sunday morning with the assistance of a horse and cart, we arrived at 3 Peel Green Road - a rambling old house with a homely appearance downstairs, while the upstairs possessed a haunting, mysterious atmosphere created by large blue painted attics, creaking floorboards and old fashioned fire grates, Three bedrooms that were situated below the attics always held a somewhat gloomy forbidding darkness which was increased by the small narrow windows.

Behind the house a small garden, consisting of a selection of weeds, overlooked the Manchester Ship Canal, where Barton swing-bridge could be observed making its daily routine manoeuvres, allowing ships entrance and exit to and from the Port of Manchester which lay two miles up the river. A variety of trees were seen to flourish along the waters edge. All this was heaven - water, grass, trees, ships - how posh could one become. An outside toilet and white-washed back yard were further luxuries on our Bartonian residence.

My eldest brother John soon became eligible for the Armed Forces and influenced by my father, he also joined the Royal Navy.

Godfrey Ermen Memorial School, where education was taught and character was moulded, and for those inattentive shirkers backsides were beaten (my own backside having felt more slipper than most peoples feet) was soon to learn of the one thing which I excelled in - my ability as a fighter.

Those unwary young males who unfortunately underestimated my capabilities, were soon to discover that this blond-haired blue eyed refugee from Hulme would not take the funning of his patched up pants and darned socks too lightly and soon I had established myself as cock of the school - *Scrapper Twem*.

The performing of physical exercise had always been encouraged by my parents, and a proven asset which has enabled me to win numerous bare-fisted encounters with a variety of opponents throughout my youth.

Meanwhile, the Americans who were now our allies, had made their own invasion of Britain taking command of selected bases throughout the country in order to strengthen our defences. Burtonwood near Warrington had become one such establishment.

The Yanks were soon to introduce us to various items indigenous to their way of life, such as *Wrigleys Chewing Gum*, *Durex* - common terminology of that era being 'Noddy Bags'.

Almost every G. I. would boast to us naive British of being a kin to John Wayne or some other super-star. The nation's mothers and daughters were easy pickings for these American marauders, those chocolate chewing, Lucky Strike smoking smoothies, with strange sounding names, i. e. Willard, Richmond, Clint, Conroy - 'Any gum chum?'

In between numerous air attacks, exploding bombs and confinements within air-raid shelters, we pretended an almost normal existence.

1945, Germany had been defeated, the war was over. Aided by our allies, we had emerged victorious. The whole of Britain erupted into a festival spirit as a carnival of peace spread throughout the land. Brightly coloured Union Jacks were hung and flown across the cities's small towns and villages.

Meanwhile, the nation eagerly awaited the return of its sons and daughters. For some a joyous occasion, while for others grief and seemingly small consolation in the knowledge that their loved ones had died for our country, leaving only a legacy of memories and faded picture to cherish. Their sacrifice was our salvation. 'Lest We Forget.'

For those fortunate enough to have returned home, the fight for survival was to continue and promises of a better existence were soon forgotten as great expectations soon faded with each blundering government.

'To the victors the spoils.'

Despite the controversy following the war, life still prevailed and my youthful activities could be summarised on one hand - football, apple pinching, tree swinging and swimming in the Bridgewater Canal the local pool. A time when summer seemed endless and any kid associating with girls was a cissy, and besides girls wore frocks and knickers and did not possess a thingy like boys.

Winter time you could rely on snow, while Carol singing commenced early around September. Needless to say, my friends and I were repeatedly pissed off by miserable misers for our premature Yuletide recitations.

Sister Ethel had received an inner calling to enrol in the Woman's Royal Army so disguised as a cook she embarked on her new career. If the German forces could have sampled her recipes, the war would have been called off. Now Ethel was to be allowed the practice of her culinary arts on our peace time forces, and if they survived this gastronomical assault, it could be recorded in history as being their finest hour.

My brother William, who was now an Accountant, was also destined to wear khaki while father had resumed his previous career in the Merchant Navy employed by the Manchester Liners Limited, making repeated voyages to Canada and America, and returning home via the Manchester ship canal - Eau-de-Cologne North West.

1951. For me school days were over as I entered into the era of Teddy-Boys, Jivers and Creepers.

On leaving school I harboured no immediate plans of becoming a millionaire so I decided to accept employment as an apprentice Projectionist at the princess Cinema, Monton Eccles. Bored and mischievous I would press a certain button which would immediately send the curtains swishing across the screen during a performance, leaving the audience below in utter confusion.

My final exodus from the Princess arrived one Saturday night. I had managed to persuade the head Projectionist to retire for a pint after the first house, upon which I completely re-organised the whole show. In omitting the news and adverts and only presenting the beginning and end reel of the main feature, a bewildered audience found themselves vacating the premises at 9.15 pm - they weren't admitted before 8.15 pm, not even time for their choc ices. Needless to say, my services were no longer required.

Similar incidents were to follow in the numerous varieties of employment which I pursued, until finally Eccles Employment Exchange became seemingly reluctant to assist me any further, stating that I had exhausted their whole supply of suitable vacancies.

Not to be discouraged, I resumed my own search with grim determination. In the evenings I'd meet up with the usual crowd, exchange talk and strengthen my already established reputation as an up and coming hardcase (a phase that a great majority were passing through in this particular era) and fool around with the girls. Childhood opinions of the opposite sex were long forgotten as a new lustful stirring was apparent through my body - a five mile hike with a promise of breast feeling was considered worthwhile, anything more daring and the mind boggles.

Eventually, I did manage to obtain work with Matt Moran, a fairground boxing promoter who liked my style and decided to promote me as the Canadian Champion. Pretty smart, seeing how I never travelled beyond Manchester. The money, the beatings numerous, young, inexperienced and expected to compete against hardened veterans, who gave no quarter and asked none.

Four months later, after receiving more than enough leather and further education into the pugilistic arts I retired while my features were still recognisable. The brief experience boosted my self- confidence. I was never rendered unconscious and never failed to give a good account of myself, although my opponents were nearly always older, heavier and taller. I realise now that I must have been a constant source of worry to my beloved mother.

The Tuxedo Warrior

Chapter Two

THE SUMMER OF '52

The summer of '52 heralded my arrival to Morecambe, a Lancastrian seaside resort which was to play a very significant role on my journey to manhood.

Leaving the bus at Euston Road Depot, I weaved and pushed my way towards the promenade through crowded streets, carrying my battered suitcase and feeling alone and rather conspicuous, already missing the comforts of home.

After a great deal of manoeuvring I eventually reached the promenade where hoards of holiday makers, some wearing comical hats and singing, were congregating along the front. Arm in arm parties would converge on a hot-dog or ice-cream stand, purchase whatever shut them up and continued a more subdued course until some new attraction touched their fancy. Funny how some people manage to remain perpetually pissed throughout their holiday. The aroma of sausage and onions, seafoods and candy, rested upon the air within the proximity of the restaurants and food stands.

After passing the Amusement Park, where rides were rolling, spiralling and circling to the accompaniment of screaming passengers, I headed in the direction of Heysham where, after many enquiries and refusals, I managed to acquire a bed sitter under the dictation of Mrs. Mary Mitchum, the proprietress of Battery Heights, which in my case the emphasis on Heights was to be well observed.

Mrs. Mary Mitchum (no relation to Robert) was of demonstrative dimensions with arms like Apollo and mounds of moving fat, harnessed under yards of flowered material resembling a dress. Her tiny feet had the miraculous task of supporting her dinosauric proportions, small wonder her breathing seemed under constant duress.

At least 16 stone had to be manoeuvred here and there daily. Her jowly bespectacled face rested on heavy rounded shoulders, for there were no visible indications of a neck, whilst a red wig presented itself at various angles upon her head which through some skin disorder, was void of hair.

During the course of conversation, which she conducted in a jerky erratic fashion, the wig was seen to move in an orbital course around her head. The persistent smile complimenting her appearance was due to a technical fault in mechanical dentistry which, through some indiscretion during assembly, had been over generous and allowed the insertion of forty two teeth into the palates (which I had counted during their rest period lying in a glass) as opposed to the statutory thirty two. These oral misfits would click and clack out of synchro whenever speech was involved and would continue the mime of communication for a period after she had ceased talking.

My tenancy rules were short and to the point. No noise or fornicating, £3. 00 a week rent, paid prompt each Friday. Gas and electric meters were installed for her convenience.

The stairs leading up to my room seemed endless. Finally I opened the door and entered, banging my head on the ceiling. My room was situated at the top of the building in the conical on the roof and the centre of the room was the only place that one could assume a standing position. Any other movement had to be performed in crouched discomfort. A small sink with cold tap, one bed, small table, chest of drawers with a wardrobe, all in diminutive form of course, were the only furnishings in my dwelling. A gas ring for cooking and an electric one bar fire for heating.

The small window which looked down upon the microscopic world below was the only consolation in my small confine which assured me I was not a Space Pilot in the nose cone of a rocket to be launched.

The Tuxedo Warrior

Pigeons were a constant source of aggravation, with their insistent coodlie doing, their glazed eyes staring at me through the skylight. I was never able to ascertain whether or not they were suffering from malnutrition or vertigo. Seagulls gliding, swooping and calling were another source of entertainment to be observed from my small window, which also held an excellent view across the bay.

The floor below was occupied by two rather strange gentlemen who introduced themselves as Cyril and Victor. And at that time, being a little naive as to certain aspects and facts of life, I misconstrued their flashing, rolling eyes and limp fragile hand gestures as being a possible form of shell-shock, not realising until a female tenant informed me, that Cyril and Victor were two raving puffs.

Employment had to be found before my remaining £6. 00 was used up so I decided that the whole of the next day would be allocated to the task of finding work.

The contents of my case had been folded neatly by my mother, whom I'm sure would be worrying at home and waiting for some form of communication indicating my whereabouts. Everything which maybe of some use, even down to my tracksuit were all there within the case.

Before retiring for the night, exercises could not be overlooked. A hundred push-ups followed by squats and sit-ups, then a cold stand up bath by the sink, afterwards bed.

6. 00 a. m. the first mile was behind me and the air was crisp and invigorating. I enjoyed jogging and Morecambe Promenade offered perfect facilities for this healthy activity. The tide was running, soon the small boats their hulls embedded within the sand and shale, would begin to rise, their listless shapes stirring and creaking and obeying the call of the sea. My footsteps ricocheted along the quiet Promenade, the silence broken only by the screeching gulls gliding and dipping in gathering flocks above the bay.

The Tuxedo Warrior

I paused for a while, feeling somewhat complacent and philosophical, one of these rare occasions in life when you have the need to enquire within yourself as to what your existence is all about. Those gulls, they know the secret-the sea, always the sea.

No matter how high we reach and build, no matter how over populated we become in our blundering, prying, exterminating existence, we cannot control the sea. Pollute it maybe, control it never. The gulls know where they're safe, circling above the womb of life, the sea. It belongs to them, they are part of it, no lonely shore or busy port would be complete without the synonymous presence of the seagull.

Sweating and panting, I arrived back to where Mrs. Mitchum offered a breakfast service at an extra 5 shillings a day. Accepting her offer I hurriedly washed and changed then joined the other tenants already seated around a large table.

Cyril and Victor were perched like two Ventriloquist dummies, at one end, while a young female, who introduced herself as Sophia De-Vere (whom I later discovered as being Brenda Higgins) sat opposite relating her trying activities in the realms of show business.

'Of course you know,' she continued 'I could have been a star if I would have er . . . em . . . you know.'

She leaned over and whispered 'gone to bed with certain celebrities.'

By the looks of her, she had slept beneath many a strange sheet in the company of many different whatever she cared to call them. She was being a little generous to herself as she revealed her age to me - 21 - I thought 'and the rest.'

Her hair had been constantly molested by peroxides and other colouring agents giving it a four tone appearance. False eyelashes flicked and wavered ('any minute,' I thought, 'and they'll end up in the cornflakes') as she gesticulated and posed with each spoonful of food. Her figure was worth a second look, I noticed her legs were quite shapely too.

The Tuxedo Warrior

Cyril and Victor who'd heard it all before, toyed and played with their food, and giving the impression they had been used to better things, while Mrs. Mitchum lumbered back and forth from the kitchen to table serving breakfast-two thin slices of bacon in the company of one burnt sausage and not enough beans to make a fart. Breakfast over I returned to my room, collected my cardigan jacket and went in search of employment.

Morecambe Swimming Stadium seemed large enough to warrant the possibilities of a job. 'Nothing to lose' I thought, 'Why not.'

On the enquiry I discovered fate was on my side. A vacancy for a lifeguard come handyman was available and at £7. 00 a week, what luck!

My morning duties consisted of cleaning the entire bathing area, whilst in the afternoons I would be expected to keep a diligent observation of the activities in and around the pool. A quick demonstration of my swimming ability had to be performed under the watchful eye of the stadium's manager who found my performance and my physique most acceptable. I was to commence work the following day, Thursday.

For the remainder of this day I could acquaint myself with Morecambe and its numerous forms of entertainment. During my reconnaissance I became acquainted with Peter Danby, a 19 year old small wiry character with a bushy crew cut, large brown eyes and a magnetic personality-his occupation being a barker on a local housey-housey stall, more respectfully now known as Bingo.

Peter had a vast knowledge of Morecambe and its inhabitants, being resident himself for his mother owned a guest house up North Shore.

'Where are you working?' he asked.

'The Stadium,' I replied.

'Oh the pool. Bags of crumpet there. How many greens a week?'

'Seven,' I said.

'Well not bad. I make fifty,' he boasted.

'Christ!' I shouted. 'How come?'

'Well you know,' he shrugged, his eyes laughing, 'one for them, two for me. I fiddle a bit. Anyway, come on I'll show you around.'

He introduced me to various members of the social fraternity. The hustlers and the cabbies, hot-dog dealers, fairground barkers and barrow boys. Suddenly, I felt accepted. Peter who seemed to have earnt the respect and loyalty of so many had made me a member of his society.

Our tour finally ended in the Parisian Bar, Morecambe's number one night or day spot, which lies between the winter gardens where the Ronnie French Trio played and accompanied the resident artistes and a variety of volunteers who, encouraged by drunken associates, would render some popular ballad to a mixed audience.

Peter ordered two beers which we immediately downed. I ordered similar, though Peter absolutely forbade me to pay.

'Wait 'till you're established,' he said, 'get some greens in your arse pocket, I've got plenty. There'll be lots of next times. You managed to get your end away since you arrived?'

'No, not had time,' I replied nonchalantly.

'I know this bint,' he whispered, 'tits like two wigwams and charvers all night. Good looker to.'

'Just give me time to settle,' I said, 'then we can have some fun.'

'You bet Cliff! You'll have yourself one helluva time, stick with ole Pete.'

'Calling the waiters is a waste of time in here,' Peter moaned, 'don't you smoke Cliff?' he said, lighting up.

'No,' I said.

'Why not?' he asked.

'Never fancied,' I replied.

He picked up our glasses and made off towards the bar and tried to order, but two rough looking merchants pushed him out of the way. Immediately I was at Peters side. The spoilers, who were filled with booze, displayed fat guts, balding heads and hard expressions. Both were big made in unflattering places and out to ruin whatever enjoyment they could for anyone unlucky enough to cross them.

'Don't do that!' I warned.

'Ya what?' One of them said.

'You heard,' I said.

'Come on Cliff, forget about it,' Peter laughed. I turned away, Knowing the obvious would happen, but I was prepared.

One came at my back, the other turned his attention on Peter. Making a swift turn in a crouched position, I drove a hard punch in his balls, followed up by a fast head butt across his nose. His legs buckled and went down.

Meanwhile, Peter was receiving some punishment from the other bastard. Swinging him round I aimed the heel of my hand under his chin, snapping his head against the wall, simultaneously driving my knee into his groin. Both men were indisposed, leaving Peter and myself surrounded by an audience of management and staff. Finally one of the waiters approached us.

'Mr. Benjamen the manager would like a word with you two in the office,' he said.

'What for?' I asked.

'I don't know,' he replied, 'this way if you please.'

Following the waiter through a maze of corridors, we finally arrived before Mr. Benjamen's office. The waiter knocked and we entered. Mr. Benjamen introduced himself, shook our hands and indicated for us to be seated. He was tall and lean, his dress was befitting a man in his position, his brown hair had been combed forward to conceal his receding hairline.

'How old are you?' he asked.

'I'm nineteen,' Peter replied.

'No, not you him,' he said directing his gaze at me.

'I'm nineteen next birthday,' I lied.

'You handle yourself fairly well,' he said nodding appreciatively.' I witnessed the whole incident from behind the bar. Your not a native in this area?'

'No I'm from Eccles, Manchester.'

'You have employment?'

'Well, er . . .' I fumbled for words, perhaps he would offer me a better position with more money. Oh what the hell! 'Yes I start tomorrow as a lifeguard at the Stadium.'

'And evenings?' he interrupted.

'Evenings I'm free.'

'Would you consider working here say five nights, £2. 00 a night?'

This was unbelievable, seven a week days, tenner a week nights- seventeen quid!

'He'll think about it,' Peter said.

'No I won't, I'll take it,' I said with anger in my tone because of Peter's intrusion.

'Very well. Start Saturday evening and come early so we can arrange some form of suitable dress for you.'

'Oh, what will I be doing?' I asked

'Exactly what you did today,' he replied, 'see you Saturday.'

After leaving the premises Peter stopped, looked at me and said 'You bloody fool. You could'ave asked for five notes a night and got it. He's got you dirty cheap! You'll get your bleedin' 'ead knocked round for two fuckin lousy quid a night while that polite bastard sits out of 'arms way.'

'O.K. Its my head, so what?' I said, my ego was deflating.

'You're my friend that's what,' he shouted, 'I'll see you tomorrow blockhead, so long.'

He shook my hand and walked away. Some distance later he turned and waved. I'd made a good friend today and found employment.

I never realised that life could hold so many pleasures for me as I entered into each day with renewed enthusiasm.

My lifeguard activities offered me ample opportunity to expose my physique to sun and wind, turning my blond hair white and white skin brown. Admiring glances would follow my passage as I patrolled the pool's perimeter, and knowing this in my conceited awareness, muscles would flex and chest become expanded before an attentive audience.

The Tuxedo Warrior

What a ham!

Music could be heard from the many speakers positioned around the pool. All the greats of that era were constantly played- Billy Daniels, Frankie Lane, Nat King Cole, Dean Martin, Eddie Fisher, Ted Heath, etc.

Also the qualifying heats of the Miss England beauty competition were another source of entertainment to be held in the Stadium, where young female contestants would parade before a selective panel of judges consisting of male and female celebrities. (The male celebrities' observation never rising above arse and tit) who would express indecisive glances hither and thither. The male judges would drool over the scantily concealed anatomies of these young ladies (dirty buggers!) whilst the young lady contestants in the best theatrical tradition would try and project a naive virginal image. (Lying sods.)

Whenever there was a shortage of super lovelies, some of the local talent were asked to participate in preliminaries.

I remember witnessing one such event.

The locals were first to appear, but for one or two, I'd seen better dockers. They ambled before a sniggering audience, clomping past like infantry marching through a quagmire. Plump bottoms jellevated, whilst costume seats under extreme difficulties gave up the impossible task of confining the rear ends of these robust rarities, revealing a large brood of bulging bumfries. The judges and audience were hard pressed not to give out with loud guffaws and laughter.

Under the tuition of Ronnie French, the Parisian Bar's pianist, I had become quite a reasonable vocalist, doing a pretty fair impression of Billy Daniels, who at that period was an international heart-throb.

Ronnie agreed to try and coax Benjy into letting me perform a couple of numbers during the evening. Benjy gave his permission and the following night I was introduced as Britain's young Billy Daniels.

Dressed in white jacket and black shirt, white bow tie and dark trousers, I performed 'That Old Black Magic' in beguine tempo, Billy Daniels style. To my amazement women screamed and one actually passed out. Whether intoxicated by me or alcohol, I'll never know. But one thing was certain, I established myself as an entertainer, following in the tradition of mama Twemlow.

Benjy gave me a rise of £2.00 making a total of £4.00 per night. Thursdays, Fridays and Saturdays the bar would be heaving with Daniels fans. Christ, I was a star, or was I? How soon Hollywood?

Friend Peter adopted a managerial role on my night appearances, only accepting the best invitations for the frequent all night parties we attended where, on many occasions after over indulging in wines and spirits, I would found head down examining the contours of some lavatory pot. Exercise was abandoned, hangovers acquired, sex performed, morals ignored, mind and body subjected to gross misconduct and abuse. Meanwhile, summer continued.

Benjy upon being offered higher prospects elsewhere, left the Parisian Bar under the management of his successor Cedric Beecham.

Cedric was a short, fat, odd character with a head full of thick red wobbly hair. His body resembled the shape of a Guinness bottle supported by matchsticks, which rested on to shovel like feet. He was soon to display his contempt for my popularity by restricting my performances on stage, and ordered me to wear standard dress befitting a doorman. I pointed out to him that Benjy was in the process of acquiring a tuxedo for me before he left.

'You will be supplied,' he promised, 'leave it to me.'

He was a little supercilious mis-shaped carrot headed get.

Two days later he fulfilled his promise of a tuxedo. 'It has hardly been worn, take it home try it on. It will fit you like a glove,' he assured me.

After finishing work that evening, I hurried back to the digs, eager to find out if his assurances would be correct.

The Tuxedo Warrior

This suit had been tailored for some unproportional misshaped lump, with a 44 inch waist, long arms, hippo hips and lanky legs. The sleeves alone needed major surgery and at least 6 inches had to be disposed of.

Whilst trying on the trousers, close examination revealed a generous amount of material floundering unsupported around my arse and a further four inches of height were needed of trouser leg. However, by stitching a hem on each sleeve and performing a similar operation on the trousers, I discovered that while keeping my chest expanded and restricting my length of stride, the suit and I almost managed to move with some form of coordination similar to Max Wall's.

However, should one of these anatomical positions or movements falter in any way, i. e deflation of chest or widening of stride, then the suit and I would appear somewhat disassociated, leaving myself somewhere within whilst the suit continued to move, seemingly unattended.

I was later to learn after leaving the digs the following evening that Victor and Cyril had made hurried enquiries as to who the mysterious deformed person was they had seen leaving the premises.

The audience was unusually noisy for a Saturday night and feeling rather conspicuous in my excuse for a tuxedo, I was rather relieved to discover that Cedric had struck me off the entertainment list completely.

Friends and acquaintances made tentative enquiries during the evening as to why I was not allowed to sing and why I was walking with a peculiar stoop.

Cedric brought to my attention one group in particular that could be heard above the rest. He complained that the female singer was only just audible above the din. 'How lucky for the audience,' I thought.

'I want them out,' he snapped.

My suit and I managed to amble or glide off in the direction of the group in question. Upon reaching the table, I noticed that

The Tuxedo Warrior

one of the group was Sweed Gibson, the high diver from the aqua show, recently arrived. Word of this mans size had become the topic of conversation since his arrival, now I was about to witness it myself.

'I'm sorry gentlemen, you have to leave,' I announced in a light hearted manner. 'You see . . .' I began to explain.

'And if we don't?' A voice interrupted.

The voice belonged to Sweed Gibson. I stared him straight in the eyes and said 'There are no ifs or buts, you must go.'

This blond haired giant began to rise. His ascent seemed endless, the biggest man I'd ever encountered- 6ft. 8ins. tall accompanied by tremendous shoulders tapering to a slim waist and hips. Cold green eyes surveyed my somewhat disrumbled appearance, while I sensed a trace of amusement upon the granite features set above the craggy jaw.

'Who sez?' He snapped, narrowing his eyes.

'I do!' I replied, forcing a deeper tone.

'O.K. throw me out.' He said sarcastically.

Eager to impress, I hurled a terrific right cross which he intercepted and returned a left upper cut, which I intercepted 'on my jaw', giving me my first introduction to a fight as I glided arse upwards through a blur of faces taking tables, chairs and glasses on my undignified passage towards the swing doors.

I picked myself up, trying to adopt 'I never felt a thing' expression before a silent audience who watched with amusing interest (at this stage I thought balls to my image as my jacket flopped about willy nilly) as I returned to do battle exhibiting my swelling jaw. Suddenly, a table overturned, accompanied by a quick scuffle and fart, after which the whole place erupted into a free for all. Females began screaming, because it seemed the most fashionable thing to do on such a riotous occasion, anyhow most of these females were local brass and hard as nails.

By this time Gibson and I were engaged in unorthodox combat, kicking, butting, gouging, pulling, swearing and puffing.

Eventually, the police arrived looking stern, lawful and official. No-one took a blind bit of notice. Cedric climbed upon a table in order to lodge an appeal, though he never had the opportunity to say much-someone kicked his rostrum over, spilling him head first into the battle area revealing his chunky legs which were waving frantically, indicating his humiliation and dilemma.

The police, however, with renewed effort did manage to restore a semblance of law and order which gave everyone an opportunity to survey the aftermath of their hostilities. Dazed and bewildered, the participants were putting themselves back together, half wondering what it was all about.

In majority of punch-ups, a percentage become involved because of self-imagined principle, while others are merely fighting their way out, leaving the remainder who join in for the hell of it.

I was bruised and bleeding, so was Gibson, as policemen began the arduous task of obtaining names and addresses from the offenders. Surprising how many Winston Churchills and Mickey Mouses were present that night?

Gibson complained of bruised ribs and shins, but insisted we do it again some time. Cedric having regained himself to managerial posture, complimented me on my courage and sacked me for lack of diplomacy!

In spite of my bloody nose, swollen face and aching limbs, I managed to administer one last head jerker under Cedric's jaw - my final communication with the management of the Parisian Bar.

Mrs. Mitchum was still active when I arrived at the digs looking bloody and bruised.

'Good heavens,' she exclaimed, 'whatever happened come in 'ere.'

She led me through to her living quarters, sat me down and commenced her nursing practices on my bruised face. Her doctoring was more violent than Gibson's punches. In between her tortureous man-handling I was forced to explain the whole incident.

'There, that's better isn't it?' she said

The Tuxedo Warrior

A whole tin of plasters had been impregnated all over my face, even where it wasn't necessary, by her vice like fingers, making me feel and giving me the appearance of a prospective Mummy.

'Thank you Mrs. Mitchum, you're very kind,' I said. 'Now, its nothing at all my love. Stay put, I'll make you a nice drink,' she replied. 'You know, 'she continued, 'you remind me a lot of my late husband, he was rough and tough with an eye for you know what.'

'Ay, ay,' I thought. Peeping over my plasters I surveyed the faded framed photographs that hung like trophies on the walls, where handled bar moustached faces (some wearing bowler hats were reminiscent of time gone by and the keystone cops. My observations were suddenly interrupted as Mighty Mitchum entered with a tray of tea and biscuits.

'I see you've noticed my family gallery,' she said, 'this 'ere is my father and 'ere my brother Alfred, my mother up 'ere, died with broken 'art after father passed on.'

Christ my head was thumping. Who the hell wanted to hear about brother Alfred?

'And over 'ere, my late 'usband, the beast. I'll tell you the truth,' she whispered, 'he didn't pass away he eloped with my cousin Agnes.'

'No bleeding wonder,' I thought.

'Can't you see the resemblance, you've got 'is penetrating eyes,' she whimpered, trying to sound all girlish.

'Christ, if I looked like him,' I thought, 'I'd wear these plasters permanently.'

'I haven't looked at another man since he left,' she confessed, 'not saying opportunities haven't arisen.'

Jesus, they must have been wearing dark glasses and carrying white sticks. Whose she trying to kid?

'I'll bet you get all the girls don't you?'

'Caw, I don't, honest.' Suddenly I felt daft sat in a sex starved whales living quarters, subjected to enquiries concerning my love life with my face trussed up like a survivor from Sweeney Todd's barber shop. I envisaged myself alongside the rest of the trophies on the wall. I had to get out of this room

'Well, err, I'd better be making my way to kip, road running tomorrow you know Mrs. M.'

'Must you go now, this minute?' She said, her face contorted looking like a gasping goldfish.

'Yes, I must. Good night Mrs. M. Thank you, I feel better already.' (You bloody liar Cliff.)

'Good night, see you tomorrow love,' she shouted.

'Oh I, love is it,' I thought. Must get out of this place.

Early the following morning, I decided that a long jog might relieve me of the multiple aches and bruises acquired in last night's shindig and besides, training had been sadly neglected. Riding my face of Mrs. Mitchum's obtrusive coverage, I padded along the promenade as the cool summer rain relieved the aches and swellings on my face and limbs.

On return, scowling glances were directed towards my healthy helpings of breakfast from the other tenants.

'Some people will stoop to any lengths to receive that little bit more.' Victor said flashing his golf ball eyes.

'Yes won't they,' Cyril agreed, also flashing his eyes

'Come on now Cliff my love, eat up your breakfast,' Fatty Mitchum chirped emerging from the kitchen, flashing her eyes.

With all these roly poly eyes flashing and winking, it was like dining on a pinball machine.

Mrs. Mitchum definitely looked un-healthily different. It wasn't the bright red lipstick surrounding her mouth which resembled a foxes ring piece. Her teeth hadn't altered. Aah the wig, that was it. The purple wig. Perched military and still (for a change) like the peak of Everest, all cold and stiff.

'Well, we are done up Mrs. M. New wig?' Victor mused sarcastically. 'What shade of lipstick is that you're wearing?'

'Passionate fire!' she replied.

'That accounts for the burnt sausage,' I thought, 'she grilled them on her lips.'

The Tuxedo Warrior

Brenda Higgins (alias Miss De Vere) expressed her sympathy over my wounds and offered to help me eat my breakfast. Not feeling hungry I shared the contents of my plate between all three, while Mrs. M. clanged around the kitchen.

Feeling a little despondent I retired to my room where I could rest in silence and contemplate my next move. Sunday was a day of rest. The Swimming Stadium wasn't open today. It wasn't long before I drifted into sleep, only to be awakened by the mating call of Murderous Mitchum.

'Yoo Hoo Cliff! Are you up there?'

A heavy thud resounded on the stairs as she began her ascent. Christ, she was about to brave the heights. Her desperation for sexual satisfaction knew no boundaries and now she intended an assault on my youth.

I heard Victor and Cyril lock their door, just in case. Perhaps I could hang out of the window or hitch a ride on a passing seagull. The impossible actions flashed threw my mind. Maybe she would collapse from exhaustion and roll back down the stairs, yet she still wheezed, creaked and clomped upwards driven on by passion and desire.

'Christ,' I thought, 'I'll not have it. I'll wait until she's almost reached the summit then hit her with the wardrobe.'

Suddenly, the solution to all my problems appeared in the shape of Miss De Vere. Living opposite Victor and Cyril on the floor below, she arrived one floor ahead of seductress Mitchum.

'Cliff,' she said knocking and entering, 'could you fix the heel on my shoe?'

'Why not,' I replied, 'after all, you've just saved my cobblers, so I'll save you a journey to yours.'

'Cliff, what's that old bag lumbering up here for?' she asked

'Don't know. Perhaps she's contemplating suicide. Maybe she's going to jump off the roof,' I said, jokingly

A final puff and wheeze and Mrs. Mitchum arrived outside my door, composed herself and entered.

'Well, so this is how you carry on, you disgusting pair.'

I looked behind me thinking she was alluding to someone else, while Miss Higgins (alias Miss De Vere) just gawped, mouth open.

'I don't understand what you mean,' I said. 'I'm only helping Miss De Vere mend her shoe.'

'A likely story.' She shouted as her wig began its orbital journey, while her false teeth gave demonstrations of their versatility in mimical mime.

'Don't let me interrupt, carry on, but I want you both out by mid week. You, you, perverts!'

With that she left the room and began her descent, leaving myself and Miss De Vere looking somewhat bewildered.

'What was all that about?' I asked.

'Don't you know Cliff, she's jealous. She thinks you and I are sleeping together.'

For the rest of the day Miss De Vere proved she was extremely conversant with the sexual arts. We were bang at it until the sunset. I possessing the stamina and lust of youth she the knowledge of a wanton well laid young women of unlimited experience. Her theatrical talents may have been lacking, but her boudoir performance was academy award standard.

The harsh adamant expression on Mrs. Mitchum's face was unrelenting as I bid her farewell without reply.

Peter had already made arrangements for me to move in with him, while I managed to persuade the Stadiums Manager to allow me a couple of days off.

Moving in with Peter proved to be a little crowded restricting my exercise routine in the process, though Peter good company made up for any inconvenience.

Chapter Three

CHASER

The Recovery was the name of a small back street club situated in a small cul-de-sac some way of the Promenade, owned by a Mr. James Donovan. Mr. Donovan had watched me perform at the Parisian and approached me with an offer to work for him, paying the same money, expecting a similar service - singing and minding. He seemed a reasonable sort so I agreed to give it a whirl and the following night Friday, I turned up to commence work.

The Recovery was one of those off-beat, late, late little establishments, frequented by ardent drinkers who could never get enough. Lesbians, queers and prostitutes were amongst a variety of many other sordid assortments that patronised the establishment.

One large room in a basement consisting of a bar, piano, drums, and bass and a few tables and chairs, while a smaller room used as a lounge was available for those busy ladies of ill-repute, who love to live and live to love, to conduct their business. That was The Recovery,

An entrance resembling an ordinary front door was where I would be positioned most working hours (apart from when I would be required to sing) in the company of Barney Brogan, who answered to the name Chaser.

Chaser was a big burly American, around 5ft 11ins. whose face had taken more second prizes than a blind Tomcat in a Bowling Alley. Thinning grey hair covered his head and the cold penetrating eyes were only just distinguishable beneath the heavy droopy lids. Broad shoulders indicated the possibility of strength, while the thick, strong hands looked capable of administering punishment. The excess weight around his gut suggested that alcohol, inactivity and over-eating were contributing factors promoting this condition. I got the uneasy feeling that Chaser didn't like me. Trying to make contact with this man was almost as impossible as trying to conduct a conversation with a corpse.

Mr. Donovan introduced me to the three musicians who were conversant with my somewhat limited repertoire. However, they turned out to be three well accomplished musicians and within a short space of time I was performing songs which I never thought myself capable of.

Mr. Donovan was delighted. The only trouble that presented itself was Chaser. He was mean, petty and uncontrollably jealous.

'What's wrong Chaser?' I would say, 'Why can't we get on?'

'Cause I don't like no smart arse kid coming in here disturbing ma routine and querryin' ma pitch,' he replied.

'Listen,' I said, 'Your top dog around here, everyone knows that I'm only your back up.'

'Whose been kiddin' you.' He snarled. 'You couldn't back up a car. Just keep outa ma way you sonofabitch!'

I learned that Chaser had jumped ship while docked in Heysham Harbour and had remained in Morecambe some time in Donovan's employment. I could see that a showdown between Chaser and I was imminent. The nice approach was interpreted as a sign of weakness. Two weeks later one Saturday morning the crunch came.

Peter had come in to catch my late performance at 2.00 a.m. Chaser who was half pissed decided to exercise his dislike for me out on Peter. I watched as he approached Peter's table and followed.

'See here kid, get your butt off the premises!' He drawled.

Peter looked nervous and apprehensive.

'Why, what's he done?' I interrupted.

'Listen sonny boy, I turn the wheels in this joint, you go compete with the puffs!' He replied.

That remark had exhausted the limit of my patience. Shit or bust, I was going to hurt this man

'I'm talking to one fuckin' big Yankee puff right now!' I returned.

Peter stepped back some distance, the trio ceased playing and a sudden hush was observed. Donovan tried to intervene but Chaser pushed him away.

'When I get through with you boy, you'll only be able to associate with puffs!' He growled 'Don't no-one interfere!' He shouted, as tables were moved and positioned forming an arena enclosing us both within, while the audience could watch the whole procedure behind the protective barrier of tables. The speed with which the room was assembled to accommodate the incident made me realise that this had happened before.

Chaser peeled his coat off, rolled up his sleeves, spit into each hand and beckoned me on. Butterflies fluttered inside my stomach as I threw my jacket off and prepared to do combat. Chaser was big and evil, his looks for most men would have been enough but he was at least 48 years old, though more experienced than me, I was sure he wasn't as fit.

He feigned a left jab and tried booting my balls, I grabbed his foot, he smacked me in the nose and I hit the floor. He came in stomping and kicking. Rolling clear, I regained my feet and we became locked in close combat.

Gouging and hair-pulling were put into operation, numerous times - he drove his head into my face, his stale breath now labouring in heavy gasps. Forcing his legs apart by kicking at his shins, I managed to drive my knee into his balls. He doubled as I repeated the same action into his face forcing him backwards. Then, summoning every ounce of my strength I leaped forward and delivered a hard powerful blow to the jaw, sending his heaving weighty frame to the floor after which I commenced disposing of some aggression of my own with my feet, kicking his body as he would have mine.

No mercy was asked, none offered. He was tough and punishment seemed to feed his stamina as he recovered and renewed his attack. He was hard as clogs.

The two of us were badly bruised and bleeding. We paused, he glared, he turned and walked to his coat. 'It's over,' I thought.

The knife snapped open as he whirled around, gritting his teeth.

'I'll castrate you, you limey bastard!'

The audience were enthralled, shouting first for him, then for me.

Christ, I thought it was over. The knife had been concealed in his jacket pocket. This was out of my league - not cricket. Jesus, the bastard wanted to top me. Now I knew how the bull felt on the approach of the Toreador.

'Cliff.' Peter shouted. 'Catch!'

Peter threw me a bottle, screaming 'Smash it, use it, puncture the bastard!'

The crowd grew tense. Chaser paused to observe my action. Jaggered fingers of glass protruded from the neck of the broken bottle as I waved it menacingly in front of Chaser. My whole body trembled with a combination of fear and excitement, triggered off by this new threat which had now escalated far beyond the realms of a normal street fight.

The way Chaser positioned himself and protected his arm by using his coat as a shield indicated his knowledge of such degenerate practices. Slashing and thrusting he advanced as I backed off, swiping and Kicking in an effort to ward of his attack.

A savage thrust with his knife opened a wide gash on the inside of my right knee, blood soaked into my trouser leg and ran down my socks. Throwing the broken bottle in his face, I grabbed a heavy wooden stool and laced into him. I was mad, scared, and losing blood.

The stool crashed into his shins with a sickening crack. He screamed insults in between hops -he was hurt. Grabbing the knife hand, I put my head to work on his face. I'd got the bastard, he was going. Bending his wrist, I forced the knife inwards towards his lower body and lunged the blade forward, delivering 6 inches of steel into his thigh.

The crowd applauded and cheered, they were sick and bent.

Donavan jumped in. 'Enough Cliff, he's beat. Leave it.'

'Would you have interfered if the situation was reversed?' I asked.

'You're different than him Cliff. He's an animal, you're not.'

'What's going to happen?' I enquired.

'I'll tell you what's gonna happen blondie!' Chaser screamed.

I turned to discover Chaser on his feet again. He'd withdrew the knife from out of his leg and was lumbering towards me. Christ, the man was indestructible. Peter and Donavan vacated the area as the crowd re-gathered.

Chaser looked battered to fuck. How he could stand, let alone walk was a miracle. I retrieved the stool, no way now would I back off. Fear of Chaser's reprisal was non-existent, I was going to finish this man or die in the process.

Once again the crowd that stood on the periphery became silent. Peter looked terrified but he wouldn't leave. Donavon addressed us both.

'If the Police show up, you'll both go down,' he said

'Chaser,' I said in a quiet calm voice. 'You're good, exceptional, you proved it. I can't even imagine competing against you and surviving a knife fight, but you're bleeding bad and movement will only aggravate your wound. Let's call it quits, you made your point, I'll bow out now, though if you insist on continuing, I swear I'll kill you or die trying. I've got the advantage for the moment, you're leg can't support you much longer, and you're losing too much blood.'

'He's right Chaser,' Donavan interrupted. 'Listen to reason, I'll pay the kid up, he's finished. He'll leave town won't ya Cliff?'

'Soon as I'm healed up, I promise, you have my word Chaser.'

'Uh, I can rely on that then huh Blondie?' Chaser mumbled, his hard expression softening a little.

'Down weapons and we'll shake on it,' I said.

'The hell we will,' Chaser replied.' We'll drink on it.'

Peter sided up to me.

'Come on Cliff, get out now don't trust him,' he whispered, keeping one eye on Chaser who was pouring raw spirit into his wounds.

Donavan appeared with a bottle and two glasses, we drank whisky and finally Chaser grabbed my hand and shook it.

'Don't ever come back!' He warned. 'Next time you won't be so lucky.'

Donavan bandaged my leg and told me to have it stitched.

'Don't breath a word to anyone on how you received this wound. Here's fifty quid, take care of yourself, and remember your promise, to leave as soon as possible. I know Chaser, he'll brood on it.'

'Don't worry,' I assured him. 'I'm as good as gone.'

Peter and I stepped into the cool morning air. Another beating another lesson learned.

'Lucky in one respect,' I said out loud.

'What did you say Cliff?' Peter asked.

'I said let me lean on you friend, I'm tired, weary and bruised. What lie should I tell your mother over my bruises Peter?'

'Oh tell her you fell of the pier.'

'Will she believe me?'

'No more than she'd believe the truth. Come on.'

The Tuxedo Warrior

Chapter Four

HOMEWARD BOUND

Seven days convalescing in Morecambe's clean air and warm sunshine was an enjoyable rest after so many weeks burning the candle at both ends. I looked forward to those early morning strolls along the shore in the company of swooping seagulls, practising their acrobatics and preparing themselves, for the returning tide, which would attract inquisitive tourists who would invariably throw them titbits as a reward for their performances.

The time had come for me to consider returning home. During my convalescence period, I hadn't written to mam and by now I imagine she'd be very anxious and worried.

Saturday, September, 1952. I climbed aboard the bus at Euston Road Station while Peter waved continually until he and I were no longer visible to each other. Two hours I'd be in Manchester, my favourite city, my home.

There are two unchanging stable factors in our indeterminable lives, a mother and home. 3 Peel Green Road was like the wayfarers rest, always someone either coming or going. Dad and Hal journeying back and forth from sea, Bill and Ethel returning home on Army leave and myself commuting here and there.

These were those special moments, when all our family were together, and each of us in turn related our escapades.

When laughing and joking was a continuous theme throughout these reunions with Mam turning out her best china tea-set for the occasion.

The Tuxedo Warrior

When life consisted of a series of helloes and goodbyes, together with a few tears.
When both parents were there to strengthen family ties, becoming our roots and anchor.
When life was filled with every conceivable ingredient that could be assessed in one simple word 'magic.'
If only the truth could be told without lies,
If every hello never had its goodbyes,
If life could be born without having to die,
If only.

Within a fortnight of being home I became bored. Living in Morecambe's busy summer resort, where fresh faces were always appearing and sex was easily obtained, had changed my whole outlook on life. After earning £25. 00 a week, how the hell could I be expected to work for £4. 00 or less. I was unable to accept my 16 year old status when I had been living a young mans existence.

And besides, nearly all the girls I knew still wore long bloomers, elastic top and bottoms, real trump trappers. Produce a Durex in front of these girls and they'd think them balloons for Christmas decorations. By the time you'd penetrated their elastic barriers, either dawn had broke or the urge had disappeared. If you did manage by pure expertise to fondle a thigh, your face was slapped and they retreated for a pregnancy test.

Most of the lads I knew pursued the same monotonous routines, the Lindale or Broadway dance halls

Saturday nights, dominoes and darts in the pub most other nights, conversation limited to football, betting, work and booze.

Enough was enough. After a quick decision, I decided on Scotland, planning a working tour. Beginning first in Glasgow then up towards the Highlands. Och A.

The Tuxedo Warrior

Chapter Five

SASSENACH WARRIOR

Morecambe and Glasgow were worlds apart, a cold hostility was prevalent whenever I applied for room and board.

Even after obtaining shelter under the scepticism of Mr. and Mrs. MacNorton, it was only on condition I accepted a trial period of one week. Time enough for them to form an opinion of my character. Even though their Guest House was situated in the rough area of Patrick Cross it was spotlessly clean and tidy.

In my opinion, the majority of Scots appear to offer a somewhat half acceptance to any English person who should happen to appear on their soil of intrude in their society. Of course, historic and political factors could be the main agitant promoting these reluctant attitudes, though one must admit that the Scots are a rare, proud, tough breed of people.

I envy and admire the whole concept of the clans, a tradition upheld throughout the whole of their history, surviving countless battles on home and foreign soil, yet remaining a profound significant part of their heritage, their stubborn unwillingness to back down from trouble, their born fighting ability and tenacity I was soon to encounter.

Once again, the search for employment was conducted, only this time through cold, wintry streets, where trams would pass, clanging noisily, sparking and hissing their way to unfamiliar destinations with strange sounding names.

Patrick Cross at that time had very little to offer by the way of employment, but luckily fate took a hand once more and I succeeded in obtaining a familiar position as second doorman at the Locarno Dance Hall, Patrick Cross.

The Tuxedo Warrior

The interview preceding my new employment was more of an interrogation, performed under the supervision of first doorman, David Roberts, a heavy set man of medium height, hard strong features, possessing more scars than a barbers razor strap. Thick grey hair in fashionable crew cut style exposed even more scars criss-crossing along the temples, whilst the absence of two top front teeth gave grim indications as to the type of clientele that patronised the establishment.

'You may have nineteen years in your age Laddie, but you no have nineteen years experience. Your shoulders are no without weight, but it does no mean a thing if you have na got the guts to follow through,' he explained.

Christ, if he only knew. I was not even 17.

'You see,' he continued. 'This is a rough area. It's bad enough for me at times an' I'm Scots, but you being a Sassenach - could be bloody murder. You know Laddie, Scots can be a little daft when taking the whisky. Ya see this . . .'

He unbuttoned his shirt and exposed a huge scar across his abdomen - 'An this . . .' A similar scar zig zagged across his spine. 'Well, they were done wi' a broken bottle, an' you know why? I'll tell ye why. I would no let him dance wi ma wife, and ya see this . .'

'Christ,' I thought, 'any minute he'll be exposing his arse and other parts of his anatomy.'

The lecture was over, I'd got the job. Once again a trial period was to be involved, final words being, 'You ever let me down laddie and run scared leaving me ta cope and I, I'll cut ya Sassenach head off! Start Thursday night. If ya have no tuxedo, we have a spare one you can use. The man who wore it was a similar size to you, God rest his soul,' he said with a non-committal expression on his face.

'Oh, incidentally, one thing,' I said. 'Wages, how much?'

'Three a night, five nights,' he replied. 'O.K. now I'm a busy man Cliff. If you're still around, see ye Thursday.'

Not the most congenial of company or atmosphere to be engaged in I thought, making my way down the long staircase.

The Tuxedo Warrior

Nevertheless, it's employment. How long I could be expected to last or live remained to be seen.

When word of my occupation reached the attentive ears of Mrs. MacNorton, she expressed a great deal of concern over me working in such an establishment.

'The place is notorious for brawling trouble makers, drunken irresponsible louts. You best be on your guard laddie, I wouldna think they would take too kindly to a Sassenach warden. Can't think why they've employed you, your poor mither, I'm sure wouldna like it at all.'

'I'm sure she wouldn't Mrs. Mac,' I agreed. 'But it's only until a more suitable position elsewhere becomes vacant.'

Mrs. Mac laid on a grand meal that evening, followed by an invitation to their living quarters, where I received the full history of Mr. and Mrs. MacNorton's families, their traditions, their hopes and dreams.

All hostilities towards me that were so apparent before were long past as we talked and laughed until first light. Only then did Mr. Mac. cork the whisky bottle while I stumbled (using their terminology) legless away ta me bed, where I passed into sleep leaving the room rotating like a merry-go-round.

The tuxedo was a comfortable fit, no alterations were necessary.

'Well, least ya look the part laddie!' Dave commented.

'Thanks, I hope I live up to the suit's expectations,' I replied.

'Until ya get use, I'll stand in Reception, you move round inside. First sign of lumber, come fa me. Try no opening ya mouth, if ya have to speak try a Scots accent, that way you may last til' Saturday.

'Is that bad?' I asked.

'It's even worse laddie.'

The Locarno consisted of one room comprising of an extensively long bar, which took precedence over one complete end, whilst a stage of considerable height had been positioned at the opposing end. The seating arrangements were sparse, just a few tables and chairs placed at random around the dance area.

The Tuxedo Warrior

Flowered wallpaper covered the surrounding walls - whoever was responsible for the decorating must have been pissed up - for every third or fourth strip had been hung arse upwards and those hung supposedly correct were out of alignment - heads without stalks, stalks without heads added the original touch to this exhibition in precision pruning. One solitary strip of wallpaper was all in Reception, the final application to this artistic trauma, before which this unconventional artist must surely have been discovered and returned from whence he had escaped.

The Reception was a small confined area with a pokey toll box resembling a telephone kiosk. Mabel, the Receptionist had only enough room to manoeuvre till and ticket machine, anything more adventurous was performed with a few well chosen four letter words.

Mabel's appearance conformed with so many other boxed in beauties - heavy mascared eyes resembling two fried eggs (burnt round the edges) rested beneath a mass of hair, a cosmetic beauty spot (which change sides during the evening) and lashings of bright red lipstick administered without due care and attention, exaggerating the size of her mouth which displayed four surviving front teeth - two top, two bottom. 'Christ,' I thought, 'If her appearance is due to her profession, what chance have I got.'

After a great deal of carrying and carting the orchestra of sorts assembled themselves upon the stage. One bass, a rhythm guitarist, pianist, saxophonist, drummer and violinist would you believe. A warming up practice commenced and was to continue throughout the evening. They never seemed quite able to get it together.

'Take your partners for the Foxtrot.'
'Umcha, umcha, umcha.'
'Now a change of tempo - the Quickstep.'
'Umcha, umcha, umcha.'
This was followed by rock and roll.
'Umcha, umcha, umcha.'
Small wonder the audience turned to drink.

The Tuxedo Warrior

Apart from the persistent umcha, the rest of the evening passed uneventfully. Friday also was moderately quiet and peaceful. Saturday, however, was to be one of the most disastrous nights in my entire career as a doorman, also my grand finale to the Locarno.

Dave Roberts was edgy from the moment the evening began, long before any Patrons made an appearance. I had come to like Dave, even though our acquaintance was still in it's early stages. His strong forward manner had gained him much respect.

'Anything wrong Dave?'

'Yes, you're what's wrong,' he growled.

'Why, what have I done?'

'Nothing yet,' he replied. 'It's just that I didna want ta get ta like ya and I do and it's Saturday night, the Cameron brothers are home on sea leave. They're a bad bunch, they'll be here. I should never have started ye.'

'How many?' I asked. 'What are their ages, as if it really matters?'

'Four. The youngest is around twenty, the others - hard to judge. They're a daft lot laddie, a bad bunch.'

'We'll manage,' I replied.

'We'll see,' he said.

The extended drinks licence for Saturday night attracted a host of ardent boozers who began to congregate along the bar, accompanied by their wives or lovers. At least five hundred people had managed to squeeze in, making movement almost impossible, let alone dancing. Dave forced his way towards me.

'They've arrived, the Camerons.' he whispered. 'Stay close by me, you're sure to be their immediate concern. New doormen always are.'

Through the jostling, milling crowd Dave and I became separated, when suddenly a strong hand grabbed my shoulder and spun me round.

'Mind where ya put ya feet Jimmie,' the man said.

'Sorry,' I replied, 'didn't know I'd trod on you.'

'Take more than you to tread on me Jimmie!' he snapped, as three more rough looking individuals joined him.

'The name's Cliff,' I said, 'And you're the Camerons.'

'You're very perceptive for a Sassenach,' another replied.

'Well, let's just say I was warned!'

'Hear that brothers, we're famous!' He said laughing.

They all wore checked shirts and denims and possessed telltale scars across their features. All looked very capable of giving and receiving punishment.

'Would ya like a drink Jimmie?'

'No thanks, and the name's Cliff.'

'Is that a fact now,' he said narrowing his eyes. 'You'd better cool off.'

The contents of his glass were emptied into my face. I returned the insult with two fast punches to his jaw, he went down as a volley of blows pummelled into my ribs and face and I went down holding onto some ones hair and shirt.

As we hit the floor kicking, gauging and butting commenced amidst screams, blood and broken glass. I covered up protecting my face and head as heavy kicking continued into my groin and stomach. Although I was badly hurt, I managed to regain my feet, then with the aid of a chair, I flailed into them, opening first on head then another, while their ranks were being reinforced by others. Suddenly, Dave was by me.

'Here laddie, put this on for fuck sake use it!'

The knuckle duster is a useful tool when outnumbered and it soon began narrowing down the opposition.

Dave crashed to the floor, recovered, only to go down under a pile of bodies. All hell broke loose. Every face that appeared before me I hit. My face, hair and clothes were covered in blood. A blow from behind spun me round and I fell over a table onto the boards, then before I could recover some slimey bastard drove a broken bottle into my groin, leaving slithers of glass protruding from the wound. Blood gushed everywhere and the pain was excruciating. The last thing I remembered was a hard kick in the head, then I lost consciousness as the band played on.

Bewildered and stitched, I regained consciousness, surrounded by members of the hospital staff. Through my blurred vision I managed to recognise Dave standing over me.

'You'll be fine now laddie, you're in good hands.'

'What happened?' I said trying to rise, only to be gently but firmly laid down.

'Don't try to move,' the pretty nurse cautioned. 'We've had to insert twenty stitches into your groin. Why, another eighth of an inch to the left, you'd have been little use to the lassies!'

My head and body ached like hell.

'I'm sorry laddie,' Dave continued. 'But you canna continue ta work at the Locarno, for your own safety. I blame maself for the whole affair. I should never have started ye. Pity, because ye gave a fair account of yourself tonight. I'll make sure your paid a fortnights wages for your injuries.'

Hospitalisation lasted for a period of two days, after which I was allowed to return to my lodgings, where Mrs. MacNorton fussed over me like a mother.

'Dearie me!' she said. 'Whatever is this world coming to, you poor wee laddie. You're no returning to that awful place.'

Another week of porridge and oat-cakes passed before I felt able enough to make the return journey home. Finally, with fond farewells and handshakes, this Sassenach turned his back on the land of tartan and headed for home, a little bruised and a little wiser. (Courage can be a close kin to stupidity.)

I managed to keep all knowledge of my painful experience from my mother, who worried enough as it was, without any extra burden, and besides, there's nothing like home cooking and a mother's love to make one forget the trivialities of life.

The Tuxedo Warrior

Chapter six

THE ARMY GAME

'From Here To Eternity' was a splendid film, one which inspired my patriotic instincts, for soon I had enlisted in the Army, with visions of being posted to exotic, tropical places, where I could don Bermuda shorts and sample foreign cuisine and hospitality, and fraternise with dusky maidens beneath magic moonlight and swaying palms.

However, Plumber Hill Barracks, Plymouth, was to give me a sharp jolt back to reality. How on earth they managed to muster enough wind to blow a bugle at 5. 00 in the morning, I'll never know.

'Teeenshunn! Stand by your beds! Head up there! Stomach in! Chest out, your miserable shower! Eft, Ight, Eft, Ight.'

Every single morning.

After only two days I wanted my cards. Those murderous moments of square bashing dressed in Army denim and over sized berets that resembled large under baked muffins, gaiters spiralling round your ankles as you marched out of step, throwing the whole formation into a shambles.

Whenever I performed the about turn it always resulted in me coming face to face with the man in front. If Hitler could have observed my Company's parade ground antics, he would have doubled his chances.

However, trouble was soon to rear it's ugly head in the shape of the Battalion's heavy weight boxing champion, who took pleasure in queue jumping at meal times. He and I battled the full length of the canteen, overturning tables, chairs and diners, before finally being subdued by seven R. P.'s who broke up our bloody encounter as we rolled back and forth through the quagmire of Semolina pudding which had been overturned during the performance. Seven days detention was my prize for the non commissioned bout.

The cold, vast inhospitable wilds of Dartmoor were used for army manoeuvres and being November, the bleak wintry elements for a young peacetime soldier were very disconcerting to say the least.

A long march across miles of harsh terrain had been planned. The whole object of this military operation (all the members of our disenchanted platoon were in unanimous agreement on this) was to ascertain how many balls would freeze and drop off after being exposed to these Arctic conditions. It was too cold even to fart, let alone fight.

My soldiering went progressively worse and Barrack Room brawling became part of a daily routine, leaving the powers that be the only alternative - the Detention Barracks - where blanket rash could be contracted and was, and punishment administered, and was.

Four months later I was discharged from the Army with dishonourable undertones. I didn't know whether to consider it a victory or defeat, although my father was soon to point out it was the latter.

"The 3 miler"

"One arm push up (in sets of 60)"

"400 push ups (in sets of 100)"

"100 Sit ups"

"Eight 4½ minute rounds"

The Tuxedo Warrior

Chapter Seven

THE COMPOSER

The majority of people seem able to slot themselves into a useful position of society, thus becoming an asset in the industrial chain of productivity. However, there are a minority, myself included, which are more inclined to a shifting, drifting existence, searching, wheeling and dealing, trying to conjure up ways of gaining a living outside the normal function of society. For some, it can be a heartbreaking, trying experience, while others find the road to success a comparatively easy fruitful road.

Speaking on behalf of myself, I would come in the middle of the road category.

During the late 50's, after various lines of occupations had been pursued and tried, I became married to Georgina Curly, a childhood sweetheart, after which we set up home in a small rented terraced house in Fielding Street, Patricroft, Eccles.

Coal heaving, timber carrying and navying were amongst the many forms of employment in my seemingly meaningless existence, until our first son Barry was delivered into the world.

Now sacrifices would be made. Some form of working status had to be attained, no more playing around. The future must be secured.

Turner Brothers Asbestos, Trafford Park. This hell-hole was endured for almost three years. Through grime, asbestos dust and filthy appalling conditions I laboured on the heavy gang, distributing hundred weight bags of fibre to various departments throughout the factory. Seven days a week for £25.00 and all the asbestos fibre you could accumulate within your lungs.

The Tuxedo Warrior

Another source of income was acquired in the evenings, where my services took on a familiar role as doorman at the Majestic Ballrooms, later to become the Talk of The North.

Joe Pullam, the Director, was a self-made impresario, a show-business tycoon who had always been engaged in the entertainment business. Once upon a time Joe Pullam opened a small dance hall in Irlam which I used to frequent regularly until I was finally barred for unauthorised exhibitions of unarmed combat. Too soon, the establishment's heading was changed from Irlam Palais to Punch Up Palais.

However, Joe forgave me for my past youthful exuberance saying it would make a pleasant change fighting for him as opposed to the opposite. Joe Pullam was good to me, both as a friend and employer. I respect and admire his hard earned achievements and recognition.

Compared with Glasgow and so many other seedy establishments, the Majestic Ballrooms was easy to work. I'm not insinuating that Eccles was not without it's reputed hard cases, the probable reason was that the establishment didn't encourage those type of transgressors. Most of my duties were confined within the Ballroom. I can't ever remember drawing or losing any blood during the period of employ.

Working on shifts allowed me a considerable amount of free time, so every conceivable opportunity to make money was seized upon. Obtaining an Equity membership card, I enrolled as an extra and was seen to appear an Granada's 'Coronation Street' playing darts and slopping about the Rovers, smiling into the camera's lense, trying to get noticed.

'Follow the camera,' old hands would advise, 'get your face noticed.'

Well I tried. Whenever the camera moved, I followed. In fact, during the recording of a bedroom sequence you would have found me peering from beneath the bed would it have been possible.

The Tuxedo Warrior

However, I got the message, eventually realising that the James Bond parts and other major starring opportunities would never materialise from the Vault of the Rovers Return. So, I resigned myself to hob nobbing with Elsie Tanner, Len Fairclough and the rest of the star studded cast.

You can always spot an extra, even though he may have acquired a speaking part. Every movement he or she makes is delivered as though it were a major mammoth production. Speaking from experience of course, why I myself was bestowed with such an honour.

A complete script was forwarded to me consisting of a few thousand words, of which I had to say two words, and I couldn't even remember those on the day. Invariably they would give me the role as a dumb heavy who stands around looking wooden and menacing, trying not to laugh. Though I was never recommended for an Oscar, I made a few acquaintances and had many laughs.

A second addition was soon to join the family - another boy - we named Steven.

During this period the Beatles had already exploded into the controversial world of pop. These four philosophical fuzz heads were to become a legend in their own time. They were the greatest sensation since Elvis shook his pelvis. Their music was played constantly throughout the world.

However, during their fantastic rise to the orbital plane of fame and adoration, it would appear that only their bodies returned, leaving their minds in some terrestrial dwelling, leaving millions of admirers stunned and disenchanted, deserted without idols to scream at following their dramatic decision to disband.

One of the major consequences of life is death. Sooner or later this final unavoidable conclusion comes to us all. Only when those near and dear to you are pronounced dead do you realise its devastating effect.

The Tuxedo Warrior

The passing of my parents during this period came as a great shock and sad loss. The family now became divided, like ships destined to sail an endless sea without the sanctuary of a home Port. I never realised the extent of my love for both my parents, especially my mother who had been over-burdened with more than her share of hard work and illness for most of her life. Only in her final years did she enjoy a form of peaceful existence before her life was suddenly ended. When people speak to me of divine presence, God's will and all that crap, I feel like vomiting. How intelligent people can believe such infantile hogwash is beyond my comprehension.

Whenever I find myself led into such a discussion, I am quick to demonstrate my total disbelief in any religious cult whatsoever. If any form of God exist, then I am sure we would not have the need to be told of his existence, instinctively we would know.

For instance, our awareness of less heavenly knowledge i. e hunger, love, sex, fear, cold etc., are all natural instincts. Our creator would take precedence over and above all these common instincts without the need for us to be informed.

Imagine if such a divine spirit was to exist. The conceit of him or it, demanding worship and daily prayers and in return hurricanes, earthquakes, killing thousands upon thousands of innocent people. And this is God's will?

*

And whilst in last account,
I am besieged to confess of spoilations
Before those whose knowledge be of less than mine
Expressions of damnation and sympathetic reluctance
Relfected for complete indifference.

I am aware of nothing
Other than which I accept to be of natural origin
Example

The Tuxedo Warrior

The dawn of light transforming night into day
Yet outrageous in comparison
Take credit worthy of heavenly grace
Such laborious task performed
Creating all and everything before a seventh dawn.

Who knows of this said truth contained on withered Scroll?
Distorted by misguided hands
In mention of terrestrial form
Worshipped in conceited pose
And in return disproven immortality
Sworn guidance for faithful soul religiously unjustified
When in all of truth should destiny be credited control

C. Twemlow

*

Meanwhile, I had discovered that with the aid of a tape recorder, I could assemble or compose lyric and tune. My voice would simulate orchestra sounds, giving me an insight as to how it could be arranged. God, the noises were appalling. Um Te Ta, Deeple, Dum Rump Pa Pa! I was in hysterics listening to the playback. How would a publisher react?

William, my brother, was soon to come with assistance in the form of a guitar which he had mastered with some degree of proficiency. Look out Rogers and Hammerstein and Beatles, I was about to be discovered.

However, ten years later the break came. Two songs were accepted by a London Publisher. I had long progressed from the moon and June stage and still aided by tape, brother Bill and Tony Armstrong, a young organist whom I had also inaugurated into my musical ranks. Using the De Dum Da principle from mouth to tape, within a comparatively short space of time, I had compiled the staggering total of two thousand compositions under the pen name 'Peter Reno.'

The Tuxedo Warrior

Most of the compositions were recorded and used for incidental music, while a selection were adapted for T. V. themes, i. e. *Queenies Castle, Crown Court, On Sight*, Tic Tac Advert, Electrolux, and many more. Miraculous achievements for someone who cannot even play a musical instrument, and doesn't know a crochet or a quaver from a golf club.

The rewards were astronomical. £20,000 a year was soon to be derived from my music. My whole ideology of life had taken a tremendous leap. Never again would I eat coal dust, carry timber, bounce or be bounced disposing of some drunken nuisance whilst guarding other people's property.

The Rolls Bentley and Scimitar G. T. were purchased in time for the third addition to the family - son David had come in time to enjoy the fruitful years.

10 Stuart Avenue, Irlam was to be our new residence - a large detached house within its own grounds. Fronted by ivy covered walls, the house looked rich and magnificent, a sunken garden flourished to the rear, while a quarter of an acre of land was adjacent to the north side. An unrestricted view through the lounge window over miles of farm-land were amongst its many other advantageous properties. This was the ultimate in luxury. A variety of trees surrounded the house where ever changing seasons could be observed - Spring buds, Summer's greens and Autumn gold, there they stood, my trees like living ornamental calendars.

Live And Let Die was the title of the latest Bond film about to be released. Salena Jones had already recorded a composition of mine of the same title.

Shortly after the release, an injunction was slammed on my song and Court proceedings were taken by Paul McCartney who had been commissioned to write the main title for the film.

The Court sympathised with the Broccoli empire (but of course) and my record was withdrawn from the market. Court costs were set against me and Indigo Records, a Manchester based Record Company. It was acknowledged by certain well known dignitaries of the music world that my composition was far more appropriate for the film than Mr. McCartney's.

Shortly preceding this event, Peter Adamson, Coronation Street's Len Fairclough, approached me on the possibilities of writing a song for him and Pat Pheonix (Elsie Tanner) on the understanding that he would pay half the recording costs. I accepted his offer.

Derek Hilton, Granada's Musical Director, arranged and conducted my composition entitled *The Two Of Us* featuring Len and Elsie. It never got off the ground, through lack of exposure or whatever. (Well that's show business I suppose.)

Frequent visits to London were made to ensure good public relations with the force behind the musical farce.

London - with its high social life, where paint and powder people are forever trying to upstage each other. A world with realistic hard surrounds, accompanied by a soft centred mushy fantasising interior. Where 'Loves' and 'Darlings' walk hand in hand through a wheeling and dealing, back handing, back biting and scratching musical carousel, manipulated by a handful of puppeteering overlords who manage to pull thousands of strings to success or failure. (To the Gods a sacrifice.)

Other business ventures I had entered into, which were subsidised by my musical income and bank overdrafts, fell flat. Suddenly the future had a familiar uncertainty. Call it bad business judgement, over-confidence, unable to handle success or over drinking. I think perhaps all were instrumental in the course of events to follow.

It was on this return to earth I met Judith Lewis, a tall slender red haired Jewish girl who had a sympathetic ear to my misfortune. Then, what had begun as friendship emerged into a far deeper relationship.

Bankruptcy proceedings had begun. Creditors, bankers, etc., were all screaming for blood. The numerous friends I had gathered in transit could now be counted on one hand.

Official Receivers have a job to do, personally I'd like to shoot the bloody lot. Nothing is sacred with this species of public servant. They appear to derive a personal sadistic satisfaction in uncovering your private life, they try to degrade and separate you from any sense of pride or dignity which you may still possess.

Of all human animals, they are the most inhuman, like the Jackal who hunts its quarry to the point of exhaustion, then devours it alive. These people administer justice. Likewise, still if one looks upon them as pear shaped computers like I did then one may still survive their barbaric moralistic slaughter.

The Tuxedo Warrior

Chapter Eight

THE SEXUAL SEVENTIES

The controversial sexual 70s was a conquest for the permissive society, which no longer had to confine its bizarre activities behind closed doors.

Homosexuals and Bi-sexuals could finally let their hair and trousers down. Pornography could now be purchased from the many devious seedy establishments lying in solitary seclusion in and around our cities, where patrons could be observed entering and leaving, their features concealed behind dark glasses and large hats - mysterious anonymous collectors of sensual hard core literature and film.

The sexual revolution had begun, now we could view ourselves on the job in a variety of positions and in colour too. The Church opposed it, the Police exposed it and the Government would eventually try to nationalise it. The word 'Gay' was no longer admissible in manly quarters. A state of Sodom and Gomorra was declared by the religious members of our society, who blamed the whole erotic turmoil on the Devil. (The dirty little Devil!)

Sex shops had to be the final nail in our permissive coffins, the ultimate epitome of degradation. God must have forsaken us and turned his affection to a more deserving Planet. Never mind, we still had football, where spectators would commence knocking holes out of each other immediately the game commenced.

Crime and violence had increased at an alarming pace. Murder, rape, muggings and robbery had become common everyday news, whilst the welfare movement and certain members of the aristocracy were sympathetically inclined towards the more infamous violent criminals.

As for myself, I was not entirely without sin. Bankruptcy and divorce were now an imminent factor in my disrupted disorganised life, causing a great deal of distress and sorrow to those near and dear to me. Drink became a constant source of escapism which in my confused depressed state, launched me into many a bar room brawl.

The beautiful large detached house with ivy coloured walls, surrounded by lawns and trees, was gone. The Rolls Bentley, the Scimitar Sports were no longer mine. I'd made a fortune, became successful then blew it.

After becoming accustomed to wealth and luxury, the return to normal living standards was a bitter pill to swallow. Even so, I had achieved more than most and enjoyed some degree of success which no one could deny. I had been there, lived rich and high - I made it.

1976 - a period when families consisting of more than enough children could be encouraged to live on the Welfare State and enjoy a great many other benefits on offer. Dole queues were on the increase, along with inflation. Britain's financial state was undergoing a catastrophical ebb as once again I entered into the search for employment.

Divorce Proceedings were already in motion, along with the bankruptcy.

My sister Ethel, now married to a big whisky walloping Scot named Gerrard Bellew, allowed me to reside with them along with their two small sons, at their Eccles residence, thus allowing me time to recuperate.

I looked a mess. Pinched and puckered around face eyes, loose around chest and gut. The frame was wilting, the muscles and firmness retreated under the corruption of drink, worry and fatigue. Something had to be done, a firm grip taken, a state of physical fitness attained.

The Tuxedo Warrior

The 47 inch chest and 32 inch waist had to be retrieved - either that or fitted corsets. Now began the tedious toil of ridding my body of the high life's over indulgences, the arduous task of rebuilding and shaping mind into a healthier being.

Beginning with twenty squats, three sets of twenty push ups and followed by the same amount of abdominal exercises, I soon progressed to the stage whereby I could perform one hundred and fifty push-ups on ten fingers without a pause. Eventually, sixty one arm push-ups either arm were accomplished and inserted into my daily keep-fit routine.

Meanwhile, Lomas and Baynes Limited, suppliers of office equipment, offered me employment as a van driver, delivering various items of equipment to offices and factories throughout Britain. Wherever my deliveries took me, I was always accompanied by me track suit and each day I would park the van in some quiet lay-by while I completed a three mile run.

Shortly after my divorce Judith and I were married and moved into a small rented newly built flat in Whitefield, Manchester. The flat was situated in a quiet cul-de-sac off Bury Old Road, placed within easy access to all public transport into Manchester and Motorways North and South to everywhere.

My life had now been re-shaped into some semblance of order, a solidarity had been returned into life and body, the lean muscular image once lost had been restored.

Judith had influenced my restoration to normality a great deal, always there with her reassurance of better times pending greater achievements to be made. Working as a secretary for a Manchester firm of solicitors, Judith earned a fairly substantial income which enabled us to acquire many of the necessary furnishings for our flat. Her father, Harry, also aided us to a great extent, in fact without him our position would have been almost impossible.

Although two wages were being earned, the cost of living had risen out of all proportion, come Monday mornings money was always scarce.

The Tuxedo Warrior

Numerous avenues had been explored for the possibilities of obtaining a higher income. A selection of poems which I had written had been submitted to various publishers, also a novel entitled *The Dogs Of Kane* was almost accepted by Hammer Films, only later to be returned with an accompanying letter filled with apologetic rejection.

However, all was not lost, for soon I was to appear in the infamous, familiar, knowledgeable role - no not as Batman the Masked Crusader, or Superman the Caped Wonder - but as the Tuxedo Warrior, guardian of night life, dealing out swift justice, ejecting would-be transgressors by word or force, sympathising with thwarted distressed lovers who, by fate or manoeuvring had become separated within the turmoil of night life activity, evolving within, whilst you being the soul of discretion, keep secret the knowledge that he or she's partner are behind the building having a quickie with some other obliging contemporary.

It was during the process of a delivery that I met an old acquaintance, George Maguire, whom I worked as a doorman with some years previous. George informed me that a vacancy for a doorman was available at Manchester's number one night spot, The Omega. Money and conditions he assured me were excellent.

After making a telephone call with regard to the position, Roger Howard, the General Manager, without even seeing me, suggested that I should commence work Thursday of the following week. This being Saturday, didn't allow me much time to give a week's notice to my existing employer. Still at a pinch I could work both positions for a short period.

Early evening, Wednesday, November, 1977.

Lake Windermere spread before me, gleaming and still, like a sheet of smooth polished glass reflecting the serenity of the cold November twilight that could be seen descending behind the heights of Scapa Fell. A solitary seagull glided above the grey mist which drifted silently across the lake's surface.

The Tuxedo Warrior

These moments of solitude and tranquillity which my present occupation offered were soon to be changed for the exact opposite.

Only an hour earlier I had completed my final delivery in Keswick, and this being my final day in the employment of Lomas and Baynes, I wanted to take full advantage of the situation and enjoy the peace and solitude of this cold November evening.

Noticeable signs of winter were apparent throughout the surrounding landscapes, but for the lake at least the invasion of summer was over. Evidence of her violation remained in the form of Coke and Beer cans, old tyres, broken bottles, plastic containers, all of which lay beneath in her stony shallow, yet even with all this spoliation in evidence, she still remained dignified, mysterious and enchanting. The pitfalls and problems of life seem so insignificant when confronted with the dramatic realisation of nature's impressive scenic splendour.

Time now to meditate, take an account of my life, subtract the possibilities from the impossibilities. Where am I going? What have I done? Where did I fail?

Forty one years old and returning to an occupation that can be both hazardous physically, soul destroying mentally. Depending on how you can adapt and employ your own methods of working can mean the difference between servant and master. Either you gain respect as an efficient supervisor or become humble, abused, a rubbing rag for every self-opinionated pratt you have the misfortune to deal with.

There are certain members of society who still maintain that anyone without a College education is below recognition, while statistics prove that the finest athletes, entertainers, composers, authors, etc., come from poor backgrounds and their standards of education are little more than average. On numerous occasions during my musical revolution, I had rubbed shoulders with a variety of these supremoes of society and invariably I found them to be boring, vulgar and conceited, without concern or sympathy for anyone other than themselves - a right load of wankers. However, there is one gratifying consolation born out of my adventurous intrusion into their world - I discovered that I could survive their trough, though I doubt that they could survive in mine.

The Tuxedo Warrior

Chapter Nine

THE OMEGA

8.10 p.m. The train would arrive any minute. The station was positioned high above Bury Old Road, giving a comfortable view of warmly lit houses situated below, where people had settled in for the night, enjoying the television or perhaps reading, making love.

Cold November winds which swept unchallenged down from the Pennines sent dark clouds in silent passage across the night sky. One hell of a night to stand door. The train rumbled to a halt, doors slammed and two old ladies vacated, seemingly reluctant to leave their warm, smoky commuter, complained about the cold and disappeared through the exit.

Soon I was travelling in the direction of Manchester, seated amongst a collective host of passengers - young ladies exposing their thighs, while elderly gentlemen pretending to appear unimpressed, continued reading their newspapers upside down. Directly facing, a drunken individual nods loosely in rhythmic stupor, booze sodden face, protruding belly, unsecured trouser zip, revealing none too clean underwear, odd socks exposed over worn boots, a peak-cap tilts precariously upon his head. Not the most ostentatious dresser.

Manchester's C. I. S. building made its offensive rise against the skyline as the train snapped and jerked towards Victoria Station. Everyone departed, leaving the drunken lout to burp, snore and fart in his own company.

Making my way up Corporation Street towards the town centre, I turned left and heaved throughout a series of back streets and alleyways, finally arriving in West Mosley Street, where The Omega's neon sign illuminated the narrow thoroughfare. I

The Tuxedo Warrior

descended into the reception area via two flights of stairs and made my way towards the Head Office.

There were three bars situated in convenient positions around the perimeter of the club. A unique dining complex had been cunningly arranged along the far side adjacent to the kitchen, while small cubicles of intimate design lay discreetly along the opposing wall under subdued lighting.

The dance area rested beneath a sophisticated arrangement of quadraphonic speakers and psychedelic lighting, these being operated from the D. J. stand, which overlooked the entire dance floor from an elevated position, surrounded by a confusion of knobs, dials and turntables. The whole scene was most impressive.

Roger Howard, General Manager, opened the office door and summoned me inside his spacious headquarters. The interior was of the most eloquent taste.

Large desk exhibiting typewriter, adding machine and more than enough telephones, brown cork tiles covered the four walls, padded leather chairs and mahogany drinks cabinet took position besides a large plush studio couch. (For the use of?)

Roger was of average height, very slim with fair hair, blue eyes and rather effeminate in his mannerisms. The boyish features and charming personality were used with a certain savoir-faire for luring and practising his voracious sexual skills on certain unwary naive females. His attire was demonstrated with fashionable flair, Fred Astair 1970's.

'Glad you were able to start work tonight Cliff,' he said.

'Thought it would be beneficial for all concerned to re-acquaint myself with the position as soon as possible,' I replied.

'George gave you a tremendous recommendation, says you're very useful if and when it goes off/ You're certainly the right build and you don't exhibit a broken nose or cauliflower ears. We like our doormen to appear non-aggressive, yet be able to handle any situation which may arise during the course of duty.

You will receive £70.00 per week for six nights, hours 9.00 p.m. while 2.00 a. m. although we do expect one of you will

The Tuxedo Warrior

remain until 3.00 a.m. or later, just as a precautionary measure for the hangers on in the restaurant.

Three drinks will be allowed to you each night, and any tips that might arise are your own, smoking is not allowed until after 2.00 a.m. One doorman will supervise the top door, the other below near reception. I myself will remain in reception for most part of the evening. Now, are there any questions Cliff?'

'Yes, my clothes, I don't have a tuxedo.'

He examined my dark brown suit with a discerning eye.

'Not to worry,' he said finally. 'Tomorrow we will meet in town and I will introduce you to my tailor who will make the necessary requirements for you - at the firm's expense of course. George should have arrived by now, so if you would make your way to reception, he will acquaint you with any details I may have omitted. Nice to have you with us.'

Removing my heavy overcoat, I walked back in the direction of reception to the sound of bar staff preparing, arranging and replenishing empty shelves from the previous night's invasion. Well shaped waitresses wearing daring leotards exposing rounded buttocks busied themselves amongst tables tidying, reorganising and replacing chunky glass ashtrays on shiny table tops, pausing at intervals to check their image in one of the many mirrors that were built into the decor. One or two passed inquisitive glances, making me feel a little awkward and embarrassed in passing.

George greeted me with a warm handshake. Although I wasn't too enthusiastic over working with him, there was some form of consolation in his exaggerated welcome.

'See you found it easy enough, eh Cliff?'

'You gave good directions George,' I said with a forced smile.

'You're looking good Cliff, still keeping fit?' He pushed his chest out and struck a comical pose.

'All the time,' I replied.

George was a peculiar shape, I knew this from past observations. A rather large head, covered with thick black hair which, through some error in styling, had adopted the shape of a German helmet. Above his bearded face the broad nose was

The Tuxedo Warrior

overlooked by dark protruding eyes, giving him the appearance of a rat peering through a lavatory brush.

He stood around 5 ft. 10 ins. narrow shoulders, accompanied by a flat chest, which tapered outwards and down to a rather large backside, All this was supported by two spindly legs. The tuxedo that covered this misgotten shape had been cut with exaggerated width across the shoulders, in order to compensate for the gathering weight around the gut and hip. A masterpiece of tailoring, complete with built in muscles, apart from the obvious his shirt and bow-tie were well fitting.

'What sort of exercises do you perform?' He asked with pretended interest.

'Oh,' I mused. 'A four mile run accompanied by four hundred press ups, one hundred sit ups, fifty pull ups, a hundred squats etc...'

'And you repeat this assault course every day?' He asked, lighting a cigarette as if to pollute my answer.

'Yes,' I assured him. 'Every day, seven days a week - summer, winter, rain or shine.'

'You must have tremendous self-discipline,' he replied.

He then decided that a guided tour around the establishment would be my first task in order to familiarise myself with exits, cloakrooms, toilets etc. After meeting various members of bar staff and waitresses, I was lastly introduced to Joanne, the receptionist, a small, trim, pretty, dark haired girl of normal dress. Introductions completed, I took up my position commandeering the top door, while George who had acquired the title of Reception manager, remained below.

Two glass doors were all that were between myself and the street, one door remained locked, leaving the other to serve as entrance and exit. The narrow thoroughfare which was utilised for parking vehicles had tall buildings on either side, the rear entrance of a bank on the right, whilst hotel and restaurant stood opposite. A large area facing the entrance had a reserved space, where the owners (whom I had yet to meet) parked their vehicles.

The Tuxedo Warrior

9. 15 p. m. and the only activity came from reception, where George was engaged in the obscene act of groping the pretty girl behind the desk, while at the same time glancing up towards me, making sure that I witnessed his uncouth molesting of her private parts - though from all accounts it would appear to be a usual nightly occurrence.

'She loves it you know Cliff.' George joked, 'she asks for it every night.'

I smiled, thinking that she doesn't have much option.

Ernie, who introduced himself as the car jockey, made his entrance dressed in green jodhpurs with matching jacket, peak-cap and large black gaiters. I didn't know whether to salute him or shake hands. His blue eyes were hardly distinguishable beneath the oversized hat which, when removed, revealed a thick growth of blond hair. Ernie was thirty years old and small in stature, and as I was soon to discover, big in heart.

'Ave ya just started?' he shouted in a broad Swinton accent.

'tonight is my first.' I replied.

'Ow old are ya then?'

'I'm forty.'

'Bleedin' 'ell, ya only look 'bout twenty nine!'

'Thank you Ernie.'

'Do ya do wrestlin?'

'No Ernie, though I do physical training each day, watch my diet and take numerous vitamin pills.'

'Best way ta be,' Ernie said thoughtfully. 'Wish I could be bothered doin' that, only mi wife is bad a lot, got cancer ya know, two operations, due for another soon. Got two youngens ta mess wi.'

'Don't believe him Cliff, he'll tell you anything,' George shouted up.

'Ya piss off, ya ferrett faced get!' Ernie replied.

'It's all fun ya know Cliff, wi don't mean it.'

'I do really,' he whispered. 'Yon man's a bid 'eaded get.'

'Such language!' I said smiling, 'and at the Omega, Manchester's number one night spot.'

The Tuxedo Warrior

'They're nowt but a load of wankers that cum in ere anyway,' Ernie said with a grin on his face. 'Some of em cum in ere all ladi-da, they ain't got two pence to scratch their ase wi. Tha's just a few tha's alright, ah make a few quid tips, tha knows you will too - back in a jiff.'

Ernie, went below, kissed the receptionist, pulled George's bow-tie and disappeared inside.

The first group of people filtered in, looked at me and indicated towards reception. After a quick examination of their appearance I voiced my approval, they thanked me and continued down. Ernie and George came up together and suggested we stand outside so they could smoke.

'How does it feel being back on the door Cliff?' George asked, lighting his cigarette. 'You don't smoke?'

'No. I don't smoke, and I feel a little peculiar.'

'You will at first,' he agreed, 'but you'll get use.'

'Course 'e will,' Ernie shouted. 'Wi his looks an muscles, e's a natural!'

'You better watch out Cliff, Ernie fancies you!'

'Better 'im than you, ya big fat get!' Ernie said laughing.

George, ignoring Ernie's remark continued to instruct me on certain forms of dress that were not admissible in the disco.

'Denims - out of the question - T. Shirts, overalls, leather jackets, long hair, tattoo's, earrings, you know the scene Cliff, bit of discretion, anyone looks a bit heavy. Mind you, all of these rules are subject to alteration by Roger, Peter or Geoffrey, who you will meet shortly.'

A pretty young girl entered smiling, said hello to George, who immediately began to demonstrate his self-imagined skill with women, as he kissed and caressed her, uttering something in French. The girl allowed his amorous advances, knowing it would mean free passage into the club.

'You're so clever George,' she said, 'fancy you knowing French!'

This only prompted his ego even more as he kissed her hand.

The Tuxedo Warrior

'Very Frenchy!' Ernie shouted.

George looked up at Ernie and yawned, trying to appear chic.

'Christ.' Ernie joked, 'What wi that beard an bloody big sloppy mouth, ya face looks like a polar bear's arse!'

I was unable to contain my laughter, as was the receptionist. George shrugged and went inside with the girl. Suddenly, Ernie broke out into more laughter, he'd produced a book from his pocket entitled 'Know Your French.'

'Look at this Cliff, ya know what that cunt just said to er in French?'

'I haven't got a clue, tell me.'

'Tea and toast twice!'

The pair of us were still laughing as Peter Vaughan one of the owners arrived. The headlights from his Rolls Royce illuminated the entire street. Ernie opened the driver's door and Peter emerged, a very young looking thirty six, dark curly hair, permed, approximately 5ft. 11 ins. medium build, quite handsome. Red suit, white shoes, cream silk shirt, long white scarf flung casually around his shoulders, almost touching the floor. He liked to be noticed.

'Nice to have you with us! Cliff isn't it?' He enquired as we shook hands, his green eyes giving me the once over.

'Yes, thank you.' I replied, detecting his slight Yorkshire accent.

'Hope you'll like it here.'

'I'm sure I will.'

George who was almost stood to attention awaiting recognition like a dog which had just retrieved it's masters slippers, gave Peter a welcome befitting Royalty. 'Good evening Sir, No Sir, Yes Sir, three bags full Sir.' His attitude must have given Peter Vaughan the feeling of Knighthood.

Meanwhile, Ernie, who was still outside, appeared to be having difficulty with two unsavoury looking characters.

'Any problems Ernie?' I asked, stepping into the street.

'These two fellers ah being bloody daft, want ta sit in't gaffers Rolls!'

The Tuxedo Warrior

'Who the bleedin' 'ell's he?' The biggest one scoffed, with a hard grimy expression. Their attention was diverted to me.

Both were above average height, dark greasy hair, earrings, dirty denims, heavy boots. Amateur spoilers, plump, over-fed veterans from the mouth and muck brigade.

In all my dealings with trouble makers, I try and conduct myself in a calm and dignified fashion, remaining unruffled outwardly, though inwardly the sensation is one of explosive tension awaiting release. A weakening experience is perceived around the stomach and legs and all these indications were with me now. Making an appeal to this ill-mannered filth would be a waste of time. I confronted the two of them - my hands clasped covering my groin, legs slightly apart.

'Fuck Off!'

Ernie looked astounded at my choice of vocabulary as he backed away nervously.

The largest and ugliest made his move, pivoting round on my left leg I delivered a hard kick to is face with the heel of my right foot, bursting his nose on impact and sending his dirty misshapen body sprawling and bleeding, while the other tried an assault on my balls with his heavy boots. Managing to catch his left foot in flight, I drove a hard right below the knee cap, released it as he screamed, kicked his legs from under him, driving the flat of my shoe into his mouth. I cannot tolerate bullies, give them plenty.

Roger and George arrived on the scene, Ernie had ran for their assistance.

'I'd rather you wouldn't become involved with outside brawls, as off the premises we have no jurisdiction,' Roger warned.

'We'll be back punk!' The two thugs shouted, limping away.

'My pleasure,' I replied.

'Everyone inside!' Roger ordered.

Ernie was all smiles.

'It wasn't that ah didn't think ya couldn't handle it.'

'Don't worry Ernie,' I replied, interrupting his sentence.

'You did right.'

Roger drew me to one side. 'You handle yourself very well, though I'm not condoning what you did, but the way you did it!' He made a gesture like a chef who had just created a masterpiece. 'Go inside, have yourself a drink - only one mind you.'

'Told you Cliff, not a bad place eh?' George whispered as I passed.

The news of victory travels fast, for soon I was besieged by bar staff and a couple of the waitresses wanting the whole saga - was there two or three - are you hurt - did you win - knock 'em out? - any blood? - serves 'em right - you're not forty, you can't be that you look so fit - do you train - where at?

I finished the brandy and port which I ordered, excused myself and returned to my position where I continued to scrutinise the variety of clients which seemed to multiply with each minute. Turks, Persians, Chinese, English of course now and then, Americans, Germans and Swedes. All seemed to prefer this night-spot as opposed to the many others situated within the vicinity.

'Ya get pissed in ere, ya don't know which bleedin' country yer in. Thi cum ere, buy the best wheels, get the best crumpet, we ave to call em Sir,' Ernie moaned.

'I don't call anyone Sir,' I corrected.

'Naw, but ya know what ah mean.'

'It wasn't too long ago we enslaved some of these unfortunate people Ernie, most of them equals with equal rights and are entitled to whatever respect the law permits.'

'You're on their side!'

'No Ernie, I'm on our side.'

'Howdya mean?'

'Well, put it this way Ernie, no one race of people should be allowed to govern, enslave of exploit another race. White man in his so called wisdom has throughout history exploited his fellow black man, brother, or whatever, his over indulgence in everything, the rape of the oceans, polluting extermination of wild life has and will continue to create havoc on what Scientists term as a now dying planet.'

'Ah, ger away with ya. Nowt wrong wi this world.'

'Those profound words will be repeated as we explode in a final holocaust Ernie.'

'Ya know sumthin. I like ya Cliff.'

'Feeling is mutual Ernie.'

'Cum ta think of it, thea not all that bad, these coloured fellas, the foreign bleeders!' Ernie swung open the door laughing and went to park a car.

My right hand felt rather bruised and noticeable swelling had occurred - my first night I thought, and already I'm out of action. The soreness came from the surrounding small knuckle and from past experience I knew I'd broken one of the smaller bones adjoining. It will heal, I thought, it always has done.

The reception speakers gave visitors an indication as to what trend or vogue of music the club enjoyed. You name it they had it. Nights of thumping headaches were to follow.

My introduction to Geoffrey Vaughan was much the same as with Peter, though Geoffrey was smaller and more subdued fashion wise - brown suit, white shirt and tie. There was a striking similarity in their features. He also drove a Rolls.

During the course of the evening, regulars made enquiries both to Ernie and George regarding my presence. George informed them that I was merely back-up, nothing more - as was expected from George.

Ernie's answer was more bias and elaborate. 'E chews um up an spits em out!' Making me subject to inquisitive glances from a respectful distance.

'What the hell have you been saying about me Ernie?'

'All good stuff.'

'For instance?'

'Well, the way ya laid those six blokes out tonight.'

'There were only two!'

'So, ah exaggerate a bit.'

The Tuxedo Warrior

'Christ Ernie! By the looks I'm receiving it would appear they're waiting for me to reveal my Superman outfit.'
'Would that be ya birthday suit?'
'Ernie, you're a little fart.'
'Ah, but ya like me though.'

The following day I arranged to meet Roger Howard inside the Via Veneto Mans shop, a gents outfitters situated in St. Anne's Arcade, Manchester.

The Via Veneto Mans shop are the only gents outfitters, in my opinion, who are well enough equipped with ready made fashions to accommodate the more athletic members of the community, catering more for the wedge shaped physique, i. e. wide shoulders, trim waist and hips as opposed to the outnumbering majorities of the pear shaped brigade - narrow width accompanied by bulbous extremities around gut and arse.

Under the fashionable supervision of Roger Howard, I was soon clothed in the necessaries - tuxedo, shirts, bow-tie and shoes.

Christmas 1977 was two weeks away. Already four weeks had passed since I began working the Omega. Regulars had become accustomed to me and I they, there had been no further instances of violence since the first night's encounter, touch wood.

Ernie still resembled a little jockey looking for a jump in his green outfit, while George continued his French overtures with the ladies. I also discovered Peter Vaughan to be an accomplished D. J. pulling more birds than a sex shop advertising fanny shrinkers. Many a lovely lass passed beneath him and Roger during most working hours. Virgins must have been a rarity, almost a swear word. However, if one such precious beauty did gain access to the Omega's sensual aphrodisiac atmosphere, then her chances of virginal survival were about as remote as a punctured haggis in a Pirhana filled piss-pot.

I love the whole concept of Christmas, from the imaginative T. V. ads to the decorative shops, all tinsled and illuminated, influencing a purity of mind into the younger generation, creating and atmosphere of peace, prosperity and good will to all.

Throughout the world the importance of this religious event is respected and acknowledged, even by countries torn between the bitter conflicts of war. Although being a non-believer myself, I recognise the advantageous commutative possibilities that can be born out of such a beautiful dream.

While a minority dwell on the divinity of Christmas, the majority (myself included) exercise their own over indulgencies in a demonstration of over eating and drinking, party congregating and fornicating campaign, furnishing brewery tycoons with immense profits, leaving ourselves with a communal hangover and a slimmer bank balance.

Manchester zeroed in on Christmas, now only five days away. The Omega was inundated with bookings of office and works' parties. Now one could observe the antics of those members of society unaccustomed to the influence of the more sophisticated activities of night life - the tell tale vocabulary as they enquire as to the whereabouts of the toilet, i. e. 'Where's the carsey?' 'Dying for a piss, where is it?' 'Which way to the fart house?'

The prime question always asked was one with regard to the well shaped scantily clad waitresses, i. e. 'How do ya manage with all this crumpet, I'd have a constant 'ard on?' 'Cor, look at er, screw the arse off that!'

These questions were always finalised by the inquisitive patron with the Sixty Five Dollar question - 'Don't thi serve pints in ere?' 'Whose beer is it Boddy's or Worthy's?'

Usually, their dress would be a reflection of their character, ill-fitting jackets, exaggerated clobbing heeled shoes, increasing their height from 5 ft. 6 ins. to 6 ft. 5 ins. Hair style undergone a severe attack from a short-sighted barber.

The female species of this particular group usually make an over-dressed appearance, either in a long evening gown decorated with ten million sequins all sewn on by an Aunty Gladys who became bed-ridden after being kicked by a cart horse. Or, the other extremities of tight, revealing, leg clinging cat-suits in velvet,

The Tuxedo Warrior

giving them the appearance of either an overweight teddy-bear in the process of giving birth to twin bottoms, or an under-fed ostrich about to be offended in a running buffet.

Two night's before Christmas Eve, George and I had to dispatch a couple of trouble makers off the premises. One of them apologised for his misconduct, whilst the other proceeded to give a demonstration of his footwork. George who seemed somewhat reluctant to become involved, stood back to enjoy the sort out as my opponent and I threw a volley of punches back and forth.

Although he was a somewhat hefty individual, he gave a good account of himself. Locked in combat, twisting and pulling, I realised my stamina was failing, he was gaining the upper hand as his head crashed into my face, driving my head into the wall. I felt my legs buckle and vision became blurred.

'Christ, all my physical training,' I thought. Suddenly, it meant nothing, how could an un-conditioned slob be sorting me out. Another painful blow rattled my jaw, I keeled over, he moved in driving his foot into my side. In a final effort, I rolled clear of his lethal kicking and gained my feet, grabbed his balls and hung on. This action allowed precious time to recover. He screamed as I pulled and twisted, almost dislodging his testicles, his eyes becoming glazed with pain. A savage tug followed by a smack across his windpipe which slammed him against the wall, where I hurled a combination of hard punches into his body before he finally went down.

'You nearly came unstuck that time Cliff,' George said with a disappointed tone.

'Yes, no thanks to you George,' I snapped in retaliation.

'Knew you could handle him though Cliff.'

'Piss off!' I replied.

After examining my face in the toilet mirrors, I was amazed to discover I had received very little bruising during my encounter. A lesson had been learnt from this incident. The body has different degrees of stamina, depending on which physical activity you are pursuing. My punching stamina was well below par. A method of perfecting long, hard, fast punching had to be developed if I was to survive another prolonged exhausting bout. Come New Year a punch bag would become part of my equipment, also a tougher training schedule introduced.

The atmosphere on Christmas Eve was magic. The Management relaxed the stringent ruling of the drinks allowance, so George and I entered into the festival spirit. Daft hats were worn, streamers flung, Christmas songs sung. No one was capable of enforcing the order.

George wore the facial expression of a man who had just discovered that Durex had to be inserted over the penis, and not the head.

As for myself, I roamed hither and thither, trying to adopt a sober gait, though a customer referred to my appearance as being reminiscent of a man walking through a Minefield wearing frogman's flippers.

Little Ernie was discovered in a state of total collapse, stolen kissed (pissed), his peak cap back to front with leg gaiters round his arms.

The night finally ended at 4. 00 a. m. Christmas morning, leaving behind a scene of utter shambles. I crawled into a taxi and headed for home. Judy, who had heard the taxi's arrival, was in the process of making coffee as I entered our comfortable cosy flat. Arranged and decorated to our taste, it was a welcome and warm retreat from the troubles of the outside world.

After sleeping until daylight, I decided to relinquish my sleep for an early workout and three mile run.

Snow had fallen overnight, making my passage through Heaton Park somewhat tiring and difficult. Swearing and cursing inwardly for consuming so much alcohol, the previous night, I puffed and panted up, down and throughout the undulating hills and woodlands. Heaton Park is an athletes paradise, miles of jogging areas, wonderful scenery, wide open spaces and colourful well maintained landscapes. Winter's wildlife could be seen

The Tuxedo Warrior

fluttering and scurrying about their business as I made my way towards St. Margarets gate, which eventually lead to Bury Old Road, then home for shower and shave.

Breakfast, over, Judy and I made our way to Eccles to visit my children, who during the years had grown some. Barry was now twenty and a policeman, Steven second eldest and nineteen was employed at a Warehouse, whilst David was still attending school. The children's grand-parents had never harboured any grudges and still considered me as one of the family. My feelings were mutual.

Christmas dinner was always enjoyed at sister Ethel's home in the company of her husband Gerrard and sons Gerrard and Aaron. Ethel always makes certain that Christmas traditions are upheld in the good old-fashioned way with a large tree, decorations and strings of greetings cards surrounding the walls, along with an abundance of food and drink - a Merry Christmas.

1978, the year when super fitness was to be achieved so that transgressors could be disposed of more efficiently, during my duties. My physical abilities had to be programmed so I would be able to survive far beyond the normal limits of physical endurance.

Oriental World of Swan Street, Manchester, supplied me with all my requirements. A heavy punch bag, gloves, two 7 lb. karate leg weights, wrist weights and grip strengtheners.

Working out on a punch bag in my opinion must be the most exhausting form of physical exercise. In the beginning stages I could survive no more than three two minute rounds. Eventually however, after muscle and lung pounding perseverance, I advanced to a stage whereby I could execute eight four and a half minute rounds, only pausing thirty seconds between each round. The 7 lb. karate leg weights were inserted inside and ankle gaiter and strapped around each leg, adding an extra stone to the activity of running and bar chinning, which I performed in three sets of twenty, followed by four hundred push-ups on fingers performed in sets of one hundred, pausing two minutes between sets. One hundred squats and abdominal exercises were also included in my daily routine.

Meals consisted of meat, whole wheat foods, milk, butter, eggs, cheese, fresh fruit and a daily supplement of vitamins - A, B, C, D and E, eight yeast tablets, three calcium and six kelp tablets, one multi-vitamin tablet, two pollen tablets, a quarter of a jar of honey and four large spoonfuls of cod liver oil, a maximum of thirty vitamin tablets per day. I felt and looked as fit as the proverbial butcher's dog.

Trouble, like so many other of life's incidents, seems to develop in bunches.

I was about to leave the club one Friday morning, 3. 30 am, when I noticed someone trying to force their way into Geoffrey Vaughan's Rolls.

During my immediate intervention into his activity, the man attacked me with a large screwdriver. I retaliated and screwed him against the wall with a hard pile driver, sending him to the floor unconscious. After informing Geoffrey who was malingering over drinks with brother Peter in the restaurant, we all returned to the scene, only to find the fellow had disappeared.

'You mustn't have hit him hard enough Cliff,' Peter said jokingly.

'Maybe not,' I replied.

However, the following morning, an anonymous phone call was received from a man complaining that I'd broken his friend's jaw during my attack. Also, he promised revenge would be carried out and contact would be made with my body in a most painful way. Threats being common place in this profession, you have a tendency to shrug them off, yet always keep them in mind.

The following evening, a group of Chinese customers, one in particular, had taken an instant dislike to George who had indicated his wish for them to leave. A series of karate movements

The Tuxedo Warrior

took place, this being too much for George, who disappeared before an amazed audience and hid in the toilets. With the advent of Kung Fu films etc., anyone of Asian appearance gathered a great deal of respect. Our imaginations conjure up all kinds of lethal manoeuvres (as shown in films) where one quick chopping movement disposes of regiments of fully armed assailants.

This could bear some truth though for already George had retreated without any application of force. Everyone had witnessed George's hasty departure, leaving me to suppress this Oriental aggressor who had positioned himself before me in an impressive karate attack pose. If this man was conversant with the Martial Arts (and the slanting eyes, powerful neck and thick broad shoulders gave every indication of this possibility) then I could be in trouble.

Roger Howard forced his way through the perimeter of people who had gathered to witness the main event, while every verbal effort to subdue him was exercised. The man, who was obviously intoxicated by power or recognition chose to ignore any approach to reason. I remained silent.

Suddenly, after a selection of well chosen karate shouts that sounded descriptive of a menu from a Chinese Take-Away, he launched himself towards me with a high kick, but, during the procedure he slipped on his arse, leaving his crutch exposed and vulnerable, allowing me the opportunity to deliver a swift un ethical kick to the cobblers, giving the audience an exhibition in Kung Shoe.

The exhibition in martial arts completed, everyone dispersed, leaving Roger to give George a severe dressing down on his unmanly conduct during the whole affair.

Two incidents where physical force was used within the course of two nights. Quite a record, seeing how the Omega didn't usually exhibit such behaviour.

Saturday evening - Once again I was to experience further trouble, this time in the disguise of what I thought to be five refined

The Tuxedo Warrior

females. Roger expressed his wishes for them to leave, on which they suggested he should go and play with himself.

I'd managed to coax them into reception under protest with the assistance of George, who with great difficulty was trying to accomplish a headlock on the tallest member of the group. She succeeded in throwing George to the floor, he retaliated and bit her leg, laddering her tights. She retaliated and commenced and assault on his head with her handbag.

The whole facade was completely out of hand. I tried to lodge an appeal to their femininity, picking the ugliest one, who came out with a barrage of vocal vulgarities that would have shocked a Bombay Docker. God, was she ugly, I don't mind ugly people but she abused the privilege and came out of doors.

Eventually, my son Barry made his appearance, being off duty and in plain clothes, tried to subdue the situation by producing his Warrant Card, which was immediately snatched and screwed up in Miss Prim's mincing maulers.

The limit of my patience had expired. Grabbing her enormous wrists, I proceeded to drag her mountainous shape up the stairs, while she continued hurling abusive language down my ear, before delivering a crippling kick in my pelvis, bringing me to my knees. Barry ran to help me assume a more dignified position, only to receive a smack in the mouth from this feminine fury.

Her assault on my son blew my fuse, and I erupted into a violent rage. By Christ, if she could dish punishment out like a man, then she could receive it likewise. Snatching her greasy hair in one hand, her fat legs in the other, I heaved this weighty walloper face first through the swinging glass doors. Her friends who'd rushed to her assistance, were ejected in a similar fashion. A dazzling exhibition of knickers, under-skirts and stockings were displayed as they topsy turvyed over one another in a floundering heap. (The daintier sex?)

The Omega's popularity developed on an international scale frequented by many famous show-biz celebrities, i.e., Tommy

The Tuxedo Warrior

Steele, Rod Stewart, Buddy Greco, Andy Williams, Bony M and most of the Coronation Street actors.

Peter Vaughan was obsessed with a fetish regarding fat females, describing them as frumpy. Roger gave full support to Peter's whim, burdening the door staff with the unsavoury task of refusing admittance to many a misproportionate Miss. How the hell could you discourage fat young ladies without insulting their intelligence - 'I'm sorry Madam, but with all due respect, I cannot permit your entrance because you over eat.'

Usually, it would end up in a free for all with myself and George trying to look nonchalant under a heavy barrage of battering handbags. I would rather fight England's Rugby team than refuse two or three 15 stone females admission into the premises.

One misty Tuesday morning, around 3. 30 a. m. the latter end of January I left the premises and began to drive home. Cruising down Cheetham Hill Road, which eventually joins Bury Old Road, I noticed a dark coloured Ford Capri through my rear view mirror. Whenever I accelerated the Capri also increased its speed. My J registered 1300 Viva was no match for the sleek modern pursuer, so I decided on a few un ethical tactics.

Three times I broke the traffic law and passed through a series of red lights, only to find that the Capri had done likewise. Speeding through Prestwich Shopping Centre the Capri drew alongside while its three rough looking leather coated occupants sporting Afro hairstyles motioned to me to pull over. I replied with a quick acceleration and 'V' sign and they followed me in pursuit.

Now I realise that these were the anonymous callers, keeping their promise of retaliation for my jaw breaking incident on one of their friends a couple of weeks earlier.

The roads were silent, apart from their vehicle and mine. Relentless in their pursuit, I realised that there was no way of shaking them off. No assistance was at hand and I couldn't allow them to gain knowledge of my home address, so I made a diversionary turn to the right up St. Margaret's Road, where I was forced to halt, almost ploughing into the local Scouts Hut.

Attack was going to be the best method of defence. No time to hesitate or measure up the opposition. The Capri was a two door, giving me a slight advantage - two had to use one side together.

Before the nearside door could open fully to allow their exit, I'd slammed it closed with a powerful kick, trapping the hand of one of the occupants. Meanwhile, the driver was out and had cleared the bonnet in a spectacular dive butting me in the face and jaw in the process. Down we crashed coming to grips, heaving, tearing, punching and puffing. Soon we were on our feet exchanging methods and dirty manoeuvres. His forehead was covered and marked with bumps and scars from previous encounters, he was what is commonly know as a nut specialist, at close quarters his head was lethal.

I was quick to demonstrate a few of my own specialities - a hard smack in his mouth with a right, followed by a quick boot to his knackers and a nose full of knee. A further crippler to his balls was soon to deposit him on his arse where face stomping was applied most effectively, rendering opponent number one inactive.

The remaining antagonist who had managed to free his friend's mangled hand from the car door, circled round me clumsily swiping, kicking and lashing. Evading his ponderous assault with a series of ducking and side stepping motions, I soon discovered that his stamina was failing as his fat gut heaved in and out under the strain of his weighty cumbersome attack.

I felt good, strong and confident as I ploughed in executing a volley of fast hard effective punches into his abdomen and face, leaving him gasping and bleeding from jagged cuts across his swollen features. After performing further major surgery on his face with the aid of their car door his legs buckled and he fell. The whole incident had lasted no longer than a minute and a half, though it seemed an eternity.

The Tuxedo Warrior

In this encounter, fitness and stamina had played the major role in my survival, helped also by the fact that my opponents were a pretty ragged unfit disorganised team.

Shortly preceding the battle of St. Margaret's, George left the Omega's employment and I assumed his command under the title of Reception Manager. A replacement was employed to commandeer the top door.

This position was taken by Ronnie Smart, a very amiable powerful easy going coloured guy, with more controversial history than Kunta Kinte. Ronnie was slow to anger, though when the limits of his patience were reached, his temper resembled that of a Kodiak Bear with its balls caught in a steel trap.

Standing at a height of 5 ft. 11 ins. and weighing close on 200 lb (of which every ounce was utilised when hitting) he presented a very formidable adversary for any would be aggressor contemplating suicide. His attitude (like most professional doormen) could change to accommodate the back slapping farm yarding opposite.

The reception area had much more to offer by way of entertainment - answering telephones, supervising and directing the public to the restaurant, toilets, telephone, bars and cigarette machine, and playing general nursemaid to many a celebrity.

The human wall practice is used to ensure privacy for the many international celebrities who frequent the Omega's famous restaurant, engaging me in the task of holding back hoards of drooling fans, whilst the celebrity slurped his or her soup, pretending not to notice the activity surrounding them.

Meanwhile, I would be kicked, poked, pulled and goosed, usually by silly birds caught up in their own make believe hysteria. During these exhibitions of masculine femininity I would perform a few of my own retaliative moves against those over exuberant females who, with disarming smile, would introduce their bony knee into your wedding tackle. Yes, many

The Tuxedo Warrior

a fair damsel has been bewinded by my blunt elbow or toes flattened with my size nine and a halfs. (The little monsters.)

The Omega's restaurant is serviced by the Italian Connection. Italian influence always promotes a touch of class and romantic glamour to our Anglo Lancastrian culinary society. The Omega is proud of its Little Italy, where broken English is exercised to its full advantage in between the burps and beckoning of the customers.

Drink, as I stated earlier, has the habit of producing the real you. If people could only see themselves after over indulging in the evils of spirit as others do.

The females, and not only the minority, are far worse than males, making their dignified entrance, poised, sophisticated, with hair arranged meticulously, like angels on a visitation from Heaven. However, two hours later a noticeable transformation has taken place. The elegant dainty step changed into a hiker's humpty dumpty gait, hair completely disorientated, resembling a wig that has almost survived a ride in a spin dryer.

Language as follows, i.e., 'Ave broke the bleedin' 'eel of mi shoe.' 'I feel pissed up Rebecca, mi Dad will kill mi.' 'I'm knackered Gladys, phone a bloody cab.' 'He's only after one thing.' 'Well, givvit 'im.' 'Whatcha think I am?' 'Ya no bleedin' virgin, that's fa sure.' 'Hey, you, ya cheeky sod, shirrup, he'll 'ear ya.'

One drink is a sedative, two an aphrodisiac, while three becomes a truth drug. Cheers.

The Omega's popularity showed no signs of diminishing, even those inquisitive undesirables who were discreetly discouraged would return days later presenting a different image - hair styled, fashionable clothes - minus earrings, tattoos hidden.

Peter Vaughan is always adamant about appearances.

'I would rather have ten beautiful trendy people on the premises and run at a loss, as opposed to a disco full of unsuitable ill-mannered yobs,' he would quote.

The Tuxedo Warrior

Although, there were numerous occasions when undesirables did infiltrate the ranks of the much sought after refined.

I have given much thought to the question of refinement. How can one define it? There are people worth thousands who are about as refined as a pig in a turd trough, and yet, I have had the pleasure in meeting ordinary working folk endowed with every conceivable asset that denotes refinement, charisma and breeding. Yes, that is the word - breeding.

High breed can sire low bred, low bred sire high bred. After all, we are only a higher form of animal, without insulting the other animals of course.

On many occasions when some over dressed female debutante would try undermining my intelligence to amuse herself (while her husband or whatever was parking the Rolls), I would console myself by forming a mental picture of her sat on the toilet, drawers pulled down round her knees having a damn good heave-ho. It works wonders for the morale.

The Omega, where one can if one desires, spend an evening in the playboys paradise, in an extravaganza of plush surrealism, where machines make music and mist to surround the grating performers, contorting themselves into a sweat and thirst.

The Omega, where waitresses and bar staff work and weary themselves while the world lets its hair down and never wants to go home.

The Omega, where Peter Vaughan along with D. J.'s Brett Mason and Earl Stylo can, with the aid of psychedelics, hypnotise its audience into performing all kinds of outlandish feats, from stripping down to nudity to acquainting themselves with each others naughty anatomies.

The Omega, a disco of desire.

Meanwhile. Ron and I would be either hoisting someone out or enjoying a quick drink, courtesy of some customer, and discussing the events of the evening.

The Tuxedo Warrior

All aspects of life are featured within the Omega syndrome. Pretty young girls stagger towards the exit assisted by two or three over-rich smoothies, soon she will fall victim to a gang-bang. Next evening invariably, she would return for a repeat performance.

The more regular ladies of ill-repute would try to hide behind the cloak of respectability, though a dog is a dog, no matter how you try to disguise it. Whenever one such lady made an appearance, Ron would advertise the fact that she'd had more pricks than a second hand dart board, or that she's courting the forces, army, navy, air-force.

The Penguin Brigade are members of the elite Anglo American Sporting Club, holding their official get togethers at the Picadilly Hotel, Manchester. Inaugurating the ranks of this excuse for a wing ding are members of the Law Society, doctors and various other business officials. Despite their so called high status in society, certain members of this brigade when under the influence of drink, conduct themselves in a manner more befitting drunken delinquents.

More often than not, they arrive three sheets to the wind, looking rather like misshaped doormen in their tuxedos. The receptionist becomes target for their supercilious attitude as they try to talk a free admission by giving some outrageous excuse in their over accentuated marble mouthed dialect. Eventually, their insults and piss taking are directed at Ron and myself and during these early stages of verbal combat, we can usually determine whether or not they have already exceeded the recognised limit of alcohol for non-admittance. However, if our judgement has faltered and one or more manage a break through, they either become slung out for mauling the waitresses or using obscene language.

Whenever approaching such transgressors, their line of patter goes like so, as they are asked to leave.

Them: 'See here, you can't do this to me old boy.'

The Tuxedo Warrior

Me: 'Sorry Sir, you've been mauling the merchandise, you must leave.'
Them: 'But they're only waitresses damn you.'
Me: 'And they're also human damn you.'

By this time, more colleagues have formed a committee and want to discuss terms.

Them: 'Now see here, aren't you exceeding your authority?'
Me: 'No, and I don't usually waste this much time on people, especially dirty old men. Are they going peacefully or do they prefer the other alternative?'
Them: 'I'll have you seen to. I know people, you'll be taken care of.'
Me: 'For instance?'
Them: 'A good hiding, maybe a leg broken!'
Me: Clout! Wham! Thump!
Them: 'See here, he didn't deserve that!'

Ron, anticipating the action, has already hoisted a couple more off the premises, and usually still holds another by the arse of his pants. Threats of violence are bestowed upon us with promise of a lawful foreclosure of the Omega and yakety yak, etc., etc. If their wives only knew one half. I dread to think! The following week or month, they will return for more sport. Hence - the Anglo American Sporting Club.

Man can make the money, though money can't make the man. Admitted, it can buy him privileges, but breeding is something within inherited from generations of copulating and crossbreeding. During the process, certain weaknesses and deficiencies can be conceived and passed on to the offspring along with a few attributes that make the coward or courageous, the refined or the uncouth.

The Tuxedo Warrior

Although the finer qualities may be concealed by a rough exterior due to the environments to which the unfortunate well bred is accustomed, given time, he will find his place in a society, who, if intelligent enough, will recognise his or her rare breed and quality.

Peter and Geoffrey Vaughan are endowed with such qualities, through sheer perseverance, they have survived and succeeded in an exceptionally hard profession. Beginning with little more than a record player and rented Church Hall, they climbed from the dark abyss of poverty and built a reputable disco empire, becoming a couple of extroverts, jet setting the world. The midas touch is just one aspect of their persona that makes them unique in a business where thousands have failed and millions are lost.

The Tuxedo Warriors are the backbone, the fibre and foundations on which such people build their empires. Without good supervision even the best establishment can fall victim to the criminal elements of society, becoming clip-joints or markets for drug pushers and pimps. Many a courageous doorman has been maimed for life and sometimes killed in the performance of his duty.

Entertainment establishments, where organised crime has been allowed to establish itself, demanding payments for protection and dealing out terrible injustice to those courageous enough to lay their life and business in jeopardy, such places present a doorman's nightmare.

Often, in these circumstances, you are up against unknown quantities. You beat one, more take their place. Acid, knives, shotguns are just a few of the tools you are confronted with. The decision is then yours, either back off and look for a less hazardous establishment, or lose all principles and degenerate to the use of similar methods.

Contrary to what the public may think, not all doormen are cauliflowered eared, broken nosed bruisers using their authority to bash a few bodies just for the hell of it.

The Tuxedo Warrior

Speaking for myself and for many others, I'm sure, a great deal of tolerance has to be exercised at all times, only using force as a last resort.

Manchester, like any other city has its villains, hardcases, and other criminal aspects. Villains and hardcases are only as villainous and as hard as society allows. No matter how hard you make yourself out to be, there is always someone willing to accommodate you and prove otherwise, and it isn't always and opponent who moves in your circle.

I have witnessed many self-opinionated hardcase who has been toppled by an enraged husband protecting his wife from their suggestive vulgarities. This species of male doesn't give a damn about villainous status, he is only concerned with the fact that his wife has been goosed and someone's going to have his balls kicked in.

The Omega has similar occurrences now and then. Jealous husband, wanton wife, hairy chested rugged adonis forcing his attention. Husband twigs on, clouts hairy chest in his hairy balls and off it goes. You dive in to subdue the affray, end up with someone's wife hitching a ride on your back and bouncing her handbag off you bonce, whilst the husband tries strangling you with the aid of your own bow-tie.

The Omega phenomena has in some respects developed into a cult, embraced by fashionable followers and posers, match stalk female models and blase middle aged sugar daddies, who, with the aid of large bank balances, try to recapture the sweet bird of youth, that is until the bedroom sequences, only then do they regain middle aged reality. (Gasp!)

Situated in a small obscure back street in the city centre, one may wonder how the Omega's popularity developed at all in an area notorious for flashers, bashers and smashers, where after midnight winos, tramps and trollops appear to emerge from out of the brickwork, living their bizarre existence drifting like spectres amongst the bright lights, noise and glamour.

The Tuxedo Warrior

West Moseley Street, nicknamed Rolls Royce Alley, is always a hive of activity from 9.00 p.m. until 3.00 a.m. then silence, leaving an empty street void of noisy engines, flashing light, laughing crowds.

The drive home along quiet roads as dawn begins to filter through the darkness is a different world, where stray dogs and cats search and wander through their lonely existence. Your eyes feel heavy and irritated by constant exposure to cigarette smoke and foul air, finally home.

The usual procedure as I arrive home is first a shower to rid myself of smoky odour, then a bloody big jam buttie, glass of milk, feet up, unwind and sometimes ponder on the mysteries of life. Upon finding life and its mysteries too difficult to comprehend, I usually retire.

Christmas 1978 came with decorative cheer and goodwill and a good time was had by all. Repeats of last year's resolutions resounded after the usual aftermath, i.e., 'Never again!' 'I'm giving up drinking,' 'Sex is over-rated.' 'I'll not participate in next year's propaganda, it's all a racket.'

Of course, all these self-promised restrictions are made whilst emptying the contents of a brandy or whisky (or any other powerful brew they prefer) down their gullets.

Meanwhile, Ron and myself listen and watch with amusement as Christmas's self-confessed sinners continue to serve or be served. No excuse is necessary for them to enjoy their favourite pleasure - every day is Christmas.

Christmas festivities in some areas seem to influence those rather restrictive practices like those first introductions into kinky capers, where stripsies and swopsies are enjoyed and under-privileged wives learn that some men have wopsies.

The ladies of this copulating cult emerge with a new lease on life, while some of the male participants, after discovering their inadequacies (upon observing Boastful Bert's giant jerker) look withdrawn, depressed and insecure, leaving only the female half satisfied, while a high proportion of the males (who usually begin

The Tuxedo Warrior

the whole charade anyhow) are left totally disillusioned and dejected.

'If you can't compete, don't enter the contest. What say you Ron?'

'I agree Cliff.'

'Are you speaking from experience Ron?'

'Naw, I got no competition.'

1979 so far has been a very good year. I remained in good health and continued my daily exercise routine.

Peter and Geoffrey had fixed their sights on London with a view to opening another successor to the Omega.

Ron had changed his drinking habits to orange juice as opposed to bourbon and coke.

Ernie remained as zany as ever, while Roger continued to dress with outrageous flair.

Numerous receptionists had tilled in and out and the Miss Omega competition brainwave had been perceived by Peter to exploit the Omega attraction even further, if that is at all possible.

The Miss Omega Competition was reminiscent of my early days in Morecambe. I was burdened with the task of clearing a passage so as to allow the contestants easy access to the dance area, where there would parade and exhibit the finer points of their anatomies, under the careful scrutiny of well selected panel of judges, male and female (female judges usually passed it and jealous, male judges all horny and for it - dirty buggers). Many things in life may alter, but the patter of Beauty Contestants must have remained unchanged from time immemorial.

Peter Vaughan, Stylo or Mason, would conduct the enquiry into the contestant's names, and hobbies, etc., like so.

Peter: 'What's your name love?'
Contestant: 'Vivacious Vera!'
Peter: 'And your measurements are?'
Contestant: '36' 22' 36'.
(Really, she's lying, real measurements being 32' 37' 49').

The Tuxedo Warrior

Peter: 'And your hobbies?'
Contestant: 'I speak five languages, perform sky-diving without a parachute, lift elephants on my back and mug heavy weight wrestlers.'
Peter: 'Hmm, nothing out of the ordinary.'

Although I've exaggerated the contestant's account of her hobbies slightly, some of their answers are as equally ludicrous.

Usually around ten entrants turn up to thrill the audience with their over or under developed proportions, exaggerated hip swings are applied as the male members of the audience show their appreciation by returning 'oohs' and' ahhs' as tits wrestle to be released and arses wobble like jelly on grease.

Eventually, the competitors retire to their dressing rooms to bitch and argue, whilst the judges retire to the toilets, where their enthusiasm is released in B flat before returning to replenish their gasses with more fuel from their glasses, and tote up the entrants scores.

Finally, the winners are chosen to go forth to the finals whenever, where a similar performance of the whole facade will be repeated.

Though a doorman's career can be somewhat problematical, these digressions (competitions etc.) from usual duty come as a source of relaxation and amusement.

Three physical bouts occurred around the latter end of March.

The first problem presented itself in the form of three Frenchmen wanting to regain what they had lost at Waterloo during the course of history, but they were still unable to match Wellington's countrymen. Fists, heads and feet were introduced by both sides. As usual, we emerged victorious over our common market comrades. Rolling on the floor, swearing and fighting, no wonder they named it the Common Market!

The second incident was caused by what appeared to be a Peruvian Yeti and built like a brick carsey. Well into 6 ft. 6 ins. in height, which presented his balls within easy striking distance. Luck and speed was on my side, he missed with a head jerker, I

The Tuxedo Warrior

scored four fast ones, two between his legs, two to his jaw, the final blow rendered him unconscious. One of those rare occasions when speed and timing were executed perfectly.

Finally, the third physical encounter was to immobilise me for a considerable period of time.

The whole episode was due to stupidity, over confidence and underestimating my opponent.

Ernie was having difficulty with two awkward customers who had been asked to leave. I immediately went to his assistance and after a few chosen words had volleyed back and forth, one of the agitators threw out a challenge which I accepted and battle commenced in the back car park. Ron witnessed the action but I told him not to assist in any way.

My opponent was short and stocky. Eager to dispose of him quickly, I slipped whilst in the process of delivering a punch to his face. My body crashed against the small concrete barrier surrounding the parking area, breaking three ribs on contact.

Seeing this opportunity, my opponent dived in, butting and belting, crashing me to the floor, where I was to receive a fractured skull, encumbering me with a further painful burden. My left side felt completely paralysed. Ron wanted to intervene, I waved him off, so he decided to knock seven bells out of the other piss artist who had been watching with sadistic delight on the periphery.

Meanwhile. I'd managed to gain a headlock on my seemingly vicious aggressor with my left arm, and stabbed four fingers in his throat with my right hand, turning the tables slightly in my favour. Under mutual agreement, we ended our painful encounter, separated and shook hands. (What a ludicrous incident). Normally, the man wouldn't have reached first bell, but there you go.

Roger insisted on immediate medical attention and hospitalisation lasted all of two hours. Under the Doctors protest, I signed myself out, pride hurting more than injuries. For some unaccountable reason my ribs refused to heal, probably due to

The Tuxedo Warrior

the fact that I commenced training five days later. However, months passed before I was allowed to return to active duty.

During my rest period, I was repeatedly asked by my wife and children to find alternative employment, less demanding, and hazardous and retire gracefully. Although I appreciated their concern and agreed with their logic, I could not associate myself with the person they were referring to. I am what I am.

The approach of the 1980's when crimes of violence continue to escalate and society more than ever have the need for escapism, I return to my position along with Ron my side kick, where I will remain until such time as I am unable to contend with the ever increasing demands borne upon the Tuxedo Warrior.

It is far better to be a resident

On the brink of hell,

Than spend a lifetime in a relentless pursuit of a mythical heaven.

The Tuxedo Warrior

EPILOGUE

Sadly Cliff Twemlow died on the 5th of May 1993 of a heart attack. This was a surprise to many because, even at the age of 57 he had a physique like Adonis. His friends all agree that he seemed to look better with age. What has inspired me the most about Mr Twemlow is not so much his humour, though you'll agree he was very funny, neither his dynamic character, wherever he went he was always surrounded by people who loved him. What impressed me most was the amount that he packed into his 57 years and the wonderful things that he achieved.

As well as the book you have just read Cliff wrote several works of fiction, many films, GBH and Tuxedo Warrior to name but two, which he starred in and wrote/sang the music scores for. Incredibly he wrote over two thousand music scores, some under the pen names of Peter Reno, John Agar and Mike Sullivan, many of which were used for television and film. He also managed to travel all around the world and became close friends with many famous celebrities including Holly Palance (daughter of Jack), John Wyman, John Ryan (*Coronation St*) Fiona Fullerton, James Coburn's son, the late Jon Paul Sigmason and he once spent two months living with Richard Gere on his farm in the United States. Many of his films and film scores were sold and produced all around the world.

For a working class lad from Hulme, Manchester, I think we can safely say that Cliff was a high achiever.

Even more than this Cliff had droves of friends and admirers by whom he is sadly missed.

I never even met Cliff yet his achievements have inspired me to make the very best of what can be a short life, I hope that his words have done the same for you.

Geoff Thompson

Other books by Geoff Thompson, available at good bookshops:

Watch my Back - *A Bouncer's Story*.

Bouncer (The sequel to Watch My Back).

The Pavement Arena
- *adapting combat Martial arts to the street*.

Real Self Defence.

Real Grappling.

Real Punching.

Real Kicking.

Weight Training - *For the Martial Artist*.

Animal Day - *Pressure testing the Martial arts*.

Fear! - *The friend of exceptional people*

Dead or Alive - *the complete self protection handbook* (As released by Paladin Press in the USA).

FORTHCOMING TITLES

On The Door - *Further bouncer adventures*.

Real Head, Knees and Elbows.

Ground Fighting - *Realistic fighting on the floor*.

Peter and the Bully - *Children's story about bullying*.